NATO AND WARSAW PACT
SUBMARINES
SINCE 1955

NATO AND WARSAW PACT
SUBMARINES
SINCE 1955

EUGENE M. KOLESNIK

BLANDFORD PRESS
POOLE · NEW YORK · SYDNEY

First published in the UK 1987 by Blandford Press,
Artillery House, Artillery Row, London SW1

Copyright © 19?? Eugene M. Kolesnik

Distributed in the United States by
Sterling Publishing Co, Inc,
2 Park Avenue, New York, NY 10016

Distributed in Australia by
Capricorn Link (Australia) Pty Ltd
PO Box 665, Lane Cove, NSW 2066

ISBN 0 7137 1804 8

Series editor: M. G. Burns

Typeset by Poole Typesetting (Wessex) Ltd.
Printed in Great Britain by Bath Press

British Library Cataloguing in Publication Data

Kolesnik, Eugene M.
  NATO and Warsaw Pact submarines since
1955.
  — (Blandford war photo files)
  1. Submarine boats — History
  I. Title
623..8′ 25′ 09   V857

CONTENTS

INTRODUCTION

When Germany capitulated on 8 May 1945, the British, Americans and Russians were quick to send experts to German shipyards in order to salvage as much as possible from the wreckage resulting from Allied bombing and German acts of sabotage. Examples of the Type XXI and Walther boats, together with the U-boats interned at Loch Erribol, on the south side of the Pentland Firth, and Lisahally, in Northern Ireland, were located and examined in great detail. The Type XXI was an excellent design and, had the hundred or so boats completed before the German surrender been used in combat, the Allies would certainly have had a formidable adversary to contend with.

While the Type XXIs were not used in World War Two, their design, which was technologically superior to contemporary Allied submarines, was to influence the future course of submarine boat development. However, the peroxide-fuelled Walther boats were potentially dangerous and difficult to operate and were, therefore, regarded with an understandable degree of circumspection.

The main features of the Type XXI, the streamlined hull and large battery capacity for high underwater speed and endurance, and increased attack depth, were adapted to Western and Soviet submarine designs in the decade after the war. Other features, which effectively countered Allied ASW capability, were also adopted and improved on. These included: the snorkel (*schnorchel*) – snort in British parlance – to allow submarines to recharge batteries while submerged; improved electronic sensors; acoustic and other types of torpedoes, and rapid reloading systems for torpedo tubes; anti-radar coatings; and noiseless propulsion systems (at low speeds) to improve the anechoic properties of the submarine and, therefore, lessen the chance of detection.

The idea of the 'true submarine' which, independent of an outside (surface) supply of oxygen, could remain submerged indefinitely, or for as long as the crew could endure it, was pursued by Britain, the United States and the Sovient Union. The Walther turbine, which seemingly offered the solution to this dream, was soon discarded by the United States because of its complexities and because of the promise of nuclear power. But the Royal Navy, which experimented with the salvaged *U-1407* from 1946 to 1950, continued the experiments with *Explorer* and *Excalibur*, which entered service in 1956 and 1958. However, it was the USS *Nautilus*, the world's first nuclear-powered submarine, which heralded the advent of the 'true submarine' when on the morning of 17 January 1955, she slipped her berth and signalled 'under way on nuclear power'.

New operational concepts, dictated by a combination of new technology and new submarine roles, forced the pace of post-war submarine development. Having defeated their enemies in the Pacific and Atlantic Oceans, the United States and Great Britain were now faced by the Soviet Union, a naval adversary smaller then, but driven by the same converging imperatives. The future implications of new propulsion technology, and the need for adequate ASW forces to counter the rapid development of submarine technology and tactics had cast the die – ASW had become the primary role for British and American submarine forces.

In order to meet post-war ASW needs, both Britain and the United States converted considerable numbers of existing submarines, incorporating as much as possible of the technology evolved from the Type XXI. In the case of Britain this involved conversion of the 'T' class, and for the United States the conversion of existing war-time fleet submarines. There were also many conversions of a less radical nature. As the ASW mission demanded high sustained underwater speed and greater submerged endurance, snorkels were fitted and, in the case of the US 'Fleet Snorkel' conversion the entire bridge structure was streamlined. Deck guns were also removed from many submarines. While 'conversions' were a useful stopgap, their main drawback was their inability to dive as deep as the 600-ft diving depth of the Type XXI, which enabled it to 'hide' beneath the 'layer depth' (stratum of water of different density from surrounding sea which adversely affects the performance of sonar) in the North Atlantic. (Another problem is the 'deep scattering layer'. This is a biological phenomenon consisting of a sound-reflecting layer of plankton, rising at night and sinking by day. Submarines are able to 'shelter' under this layer as it tends to attenuate, or scatter, sound waves and, therefore, afford some measure of defence against sonar. Temperature and salinity differences can also affect sonar performance.) The solution to their reduced diving capability was, to produce submarines comparable to the Type XXI; the American *Tang* and the British 'Porpoise' class were early examples. The hull of the 'Porpoise' class was successful and the design was used in the improved 'Oberon' class.

American success with the *Nautilus* immediately prompted Britain to shelve the Walther hydrogen peroxide turbine propulsion project and switch to nuclear propulsion. Work on a prototype reactor, at Dounreay in Scotland, was started in 1957, but fell so far behind schedule that a reactor was purchased from the United States for Britain's first nuclear-powered submarine. The Dounreay-type pressurised water-cooled reactor was fitted in two later classes. A fourth nuclear-propelled class has been built since then, and work is progressing on a fifth class to replace the 'Resolution' class. The new British SSBNs will be armed with the Trident D5 missiles, each with 16 MIRV warheads, and a range of 6,000 miles. As with the Polaris missile system, the major components will be purchased from the United States, but many sub-systems will be provided by British sub-contractors.

Test firing of the Polaris SLBM. The Polaris A-3 missile, adopted by the Royal Navy, has a range of 2,5000 nm and has solid fuel propulsion. The missile has received periodic updates, with the most recent being the 'Chevaline' modernisation project which cost over £1,000 million. (Royal Navy)

The Royal Navy has had no diesel-electric submarines built since the completion of the last 'Oberon' boat, but the cost of constructing and manning nuclear-powered submarines has forced a return to conventional power. The first of these boats, the Type 2400 SSK 'Upholder' class was launched in 1986.

Submarine development in the US Navy also followed two courses: ASW and strategic warfare. As mentioned earlier the German Type XXI influenced the USS Tang and her successors. However, to provide realistic 'targets' for the US surface ASW force, the first GUPPY coversions were carried out (for details see under United States of America). The large number of GUPPY boats were also considered as a reserve ASW force.

By the late 1950s the US Navy had realised that Soviet submarines would be its primary submarine targets in any future conflict. Therefore, new classes of submarines would need to combine deeper diving depth and long-range sonar with a new long-range weapon – the SUBROC nuclear-tipped ballistic rocket. The tactical requirements of ASW missions have changed little over the past few decades, and the emphasis then, as now, was on quietness and passive operation. (Details of the noise reduction programmes and of the submarine weapons and sonars can be found in the captions accompanying the photographs.) The problem of reaching high underwater speed was solved by the adoption of the 'Albacore' 'tear-drop' hull form, first in the nuclear-powered hunter-killer boats and then in nuclear strategic submarines. The hull form of USS *Albacore* revolutionised submarine design, giving future submarines higher speed and greater manoeuvrability.

The US Navy's involvement with strategic attack missiles dates from 1945, when German plans for a submarine-towed submersible barge containing a V2 rocket were captured. The US Navy's Loon missile – based on the V1 – was already being developed, but this was superseded by a programme for air-breathing rocket motors, resulting in the Regulus cruise missile. Five boats, including the nuclear-powered *Halibut*, equipped with this weapon, were deployed in the Pacific Ocean from 1957 to 1964. An improved missile, the supersonic Regulus II, was cancelled, and the Regulus system was replaced by the Polaris ballistic missile weapons system, itself a crash programme.

The 'George Washington' class, equipped with the Polaris system, were the first US Navy ballistic missile submarines. The 'Ethan Allen' class, which was fitted with Polaris A-2, were the first purpose-built SSBNs, and were later fitted with Polaris A-3. This class was followed by the much larger 'Lafayette' class which were all refitted with Poseidon missiles. The last 12 'Lafayette' boats, better known as the 'Benjamin Franklin' class, were refitted with Trident I. The Trident programme was the result of a strategic study for a long-range underwater missile system. The largest of the US Navy's SSBNs, the 'Ohio' class, was the outcome of this programme. An update of the Trident C-4 system, Trident II (D-5), which was first test-launched on 15 January 1987, will be retro-fitted in the first eight 'Ohio' boats, as the ninth unit, USS *Tennessee* has already been equipped for the system. All subsequent Trident boats will carry the D-5 system, which is also intended for the Royal Navy's latest SSBNs.

France, as can be seen in this book, developed her own sea-based nuclear deterrent force. But unlike Britain, which acquired Polaris from the Americans without having to pay the development costs, France had to develop and test her own missiles and warheads. *Gymnote*, a diesel-electric boat fitted with the guidance and inertial navigation system intended for *Le Redoutable*, was used to test-fire France's first strategic missile system. There are two classes of SSBNs and one class of nuclear-powered fleet submarines in the French Navy. France has also built several classes of conventional submarine, achieving considerable export success with the 'Daphne' and 'agosta' classes.

Germany has used her considerable technological expertise to develop several classes of coastal submarine, a number of which have been exported (15 Type 207 'Kobben' class to Norway), and some built under licence (two Type 205 'Narhvalen' class built by Denmark). Particular export success has been achieved with the Type 209 and large submarine types have been built for export since displacement limitations were lifted in 1980.

Of NATO's other members, Italy and the Netherlands are submarine builders. Italy, in particular, has considerable expertise, having built about 200 submarines for its own and other navies since 1905. The other members of NATO build under licence or purchase existing boats from other allies.

The largest submarine force in the world is operated by the Soviet Union; even this force is relatively small compared to the 1,200-boat fleet envisaged by Stalin at the end of World War Two. Mass production techniques were evolved and in the early 1950s over 60 'Whiskey' boats were produced annually. However, large-scale cancellations followed after Stalin's death, and an attempt was made to create a balanced fleet of submarines.

Soviet submarine tactics and characteristics differ from those of NATO. This is evident in that the conventional boats are, in general, faster, noisier and with a greater deep-diving capability than their counterparts in NATO navies. Soviet operational concepts also emphasise group attack to achieve a massive initial surprise. Soviet submarine design reflects this in that it pays less attention to survivability from ASW, relying more on long-range weapons and on a deep-diving capability for post-attack eavasion.

On the other hand, Soviet strategic missile submarines do not survive entirely by stealth, but also by deriving protection from operation in protected 'sanctuary' areas in waters close to the Soviet Union. The Soviet SSBN force numbers over 60 units of which the latest class is 'Typhoon', the world's largest

A US Navy strategic missile submarine (SSBN) taking on Trident missiles. The Lockheed Corporation was appointed missile system contractor for the sixth-generation fleet ballistic missile, the Trident II, in 1984. The last Trident Is were delivered to the US Navy in January 1986. Fabrication of the component parts of the first Trident II test missiles had already been under way for some time, under a \$5.7 billion contract. (Lockheed)

submarine. New SLBMs are under development, which will probably have greater accuracy and possess greater throw-weights.

About a half of the Soviet general-purpose submarine force, of approximately 300 boats, is nuclear-powered. This force comprises some 35 classes of torpedo attack, cruise missile and auxiliary submarines. About 100 boats are in reserve. Currently, Western intelligence reports indicate, nine classes of submarines are either in production or under test, and there is

evidence of a renewed emphasis on quietness, speed, nuclear propulsion, weapons versatility, and the incorporation of advanced technologies; the extremely-low-frequency (ELF) communications system deployed in Soviet SSBNs is just one indication of this.

The Soviet Union continues to develop a large and versatile conventional and nuclear submarine force capable of operations throughout the oceans of the world. New classes of Soviet submarine demonstrate marked design improvements, and there is a clear indication that the technological lead, held by Western navies, is being eroded. Countering this expanding force of Soviet submarines will remain the primary role of NATO's navies well into the next century.

ABBREVIATIONS

ABM	anti-ballistic missile
AGSS	auxiliary research submarines
APSS	auxiliary personnel transport submarine
ASSA	auxiliary cargo submarine
ASSO	auxiliary oiler submarine
ASW	anti-submarine warfare
bhp	brake horse-power
Can	Canada
CASEVAC	casualty evacuation
Den	Denmark
displace-ment	surface and submerged displacement measured in tons
DoD	Department of Defense (US)
DSRV	deep submergence rescue vehicle
DSSV	deep submergence search vehicle
DSV	deep submergence vehicle
DTCN	Direction Technique des Constructions Navales
ft	feet
Fr	France
Ger	Germany
Gre	Greece
GUPPY	Greater Underwater Propulsive Power Project
hp	horse-power
HTP	high-test peroxide (hydrogen peroxide turbine)
HTV	hull test vehicle – nuclear propulsion (formerly NR-2)
in	inch(es)
It	Italy
IXSS	miscellaneous unclassified submarine (dockside trainer)
length	overall length given in feet
LPSS	amphibious transport submarine
MARV	manoeuvrable re-entry vehicle
MIRV	multiple independently-targetable re-entry vehicle
mm	millimetres
MoD	Ministry of Defence (UK)
MRV	multiple re-entry vehicle
MSBS	mer sol balistique strategique
N	Neverthelands
NATO	North Atlantic Treaty Organisation
nm	nautical miles
Por	Portugal
PUFFS	passive underwater fire control system
SALT	Strategic Arms Limitations Talks
SABU	small battle unit (sumbmarine midway in size between Chariots and midgets)
shp	shaft horse-power
SLAM	submarine launched anti-aircraft missile
SLBM	submarine launched ballistic missile
SLCM	sea-launched cruise missile
SM	submarine minelayer
SOUP	Submarine Operational Update Programme
SS	submarine
SSA	cargo submarine
SSBN	ballistic missile submarine (nuclear)
SSG	guided cruise missile submarine
SSGN	nuclear-powered cruise missile submarine
SSK	hunter-killer submarine
SSM	submarine minelayer
SSN	submarine (nuclear-powered)
SSO	submarine oiler
SSP	submarine transport
SSR	radar picket submarine
SSRN	radar picket submarine (nuclear-powered)
SST	target and training submarine
SUBACS	submarine advanced combat systems
SUBROC	Submarine Rocket Programme
UK	United Kingdom
USA	United States of America
USSR	Union of Soviet Socialist Republics

1

**BLANDFORD WAR
PHOTO-FILES**

FRANCE

1. *Roland Morillot* (ex-*U-2518*) was launched in October 1944, with a displacement of 1,620 tons and was stricken from the active list in 1968. The design of this Type XX boat had considerable influence on subsequent French construction. The transfer of six U-boats to France in 1946, a Type IXB, a Type IXC, two Type VIICs and a Type XXI, precipitated the disposal of seven remaining pre-war French boats. A second Type IXB (*U-129*) was cannabilised for spares. (Wright and Logan)

2. *Sibylle* (S 614) (ex-*Sportsman*, 'S class, 3rd group) one of four 'S' class submarines acquired from Britain in 1951 on a four-year loan, extended for the remaining three boats after the accidental loss of *Sibylle* in September 1952. The remaining three boats, rated as 'Saphir' class training boats, were returned to Britain between 1958 and 1961. (Wright and Logan)

1

2

3. *La Creole* (S 606) lead vessel of this five-boat class, consisting of uncompleted 'Aurore' type submarines laid down in the late 1930s but completed from 1949 to 1954. The last boat, *L'Artemis* (S 603), was stricken in 1967. (M. Bar)

4. *Narval* (S 631), lead boat of this class of six patrol submarines was laid down in 1951, launched in 1954 and completed in 1957. The design of these boats was heavily influenced by experience with the Type XXI *Roland Morillot*; in reality they are improved Type XXIs with similar measurements and displacement but better performance. Its dimensions are: length 257 ft; beam 26 ft; and draught 17 ft. Its displacements is 1,635 tons surfaced and 1,190 tons submerged. Two Schneider diesels plus two electric motors produce 4,400 bhp/5,000 shp, giving a maximum speed of 18 knots. The range is 15,000 nautical miles at eight knots snorting. Armament consists of six bow and two stern 550 mm torpedo tubes. Only two of this class remain in service. (Marine Nationale)

3

4

5. *Amazone* (639), an 'Arethuse' class attack submarine. None of this class of four boats remains in service. Launched from 1957 to 1958, these were the world's first hunter-killer submarines. They were also the first submarines to have diesel-electric propulsion. Its displacement was 543 tons surfaced and 669 submerged. Its dimensions were: length 163 ft;

beam 19 ft; and draught 13 ft. (Marine Nationale)

6. Only nine 'Daphne' class boats remain in service from a total of 111. They displace 869 tons surfaced and 1,043 tons submerged. Their dimensions are: length 190 ft; beam 22 ft; and draught 15 ft. Maximum speed is 16 knots and

the range is 4,500 nm at 5 knots. Armament consists of eight bow and four stern 550 mm torpedo tubes. The electronics and weapons fits were modernised from 1971 onwards. Several boats had a prominent sonar dome fitted above the bow, as is shown on Daphne (S 641). (ECP Armees)

5

6

7

7. *Gymnote*, France's experimental ballistic missile submarine, was launched in 1964, the product of studies in the mid 1950s for a nuclear-powered submarine. It was intended that the boat would have a reactor using enriched uranium but as the French were unable to produce this, the only solution was to use unrefined uranium. However, as the US would not sell France either enriched uranium or a suitable reactor, the boat was completed as a conventional diesel-electric submarine with four ballistic missile tubes. (ECP Armees)

8. *Gymnote* displaces 3,000 tons surfaced and 3,250 tons submerged. Its dimensions are: length 276 ft; beam 35 ft; and draught 25 ft. Power is provided by SEMT-Pielstic diesels and two electric motors. Its top speed is about 11 kots. (ECP Armees)

8

9. The 'Le Redoutable' class nuclear-powered ballistic missile submarine *Le Terrible* (S 612), launched in 1969. This class of six was launched between 1967 and 1982, as their construction posed a number of technical problems, such as the adaption of the hull for nuclear propulsion and the development of high-tensile steel to withstand the increased diving depth. The machinery includes one pressurised water-cooled nuclear reactor, two turbines plus turbo-alternators and one electric motor. There is also an auxiliary emergency diesel, rated at 2,760 bhp. (ECP Armees)

10. *Le Terrible* is armed with 16 tubes for the MSBS M-20 nuclear missile and has four 550 mm bow torpedo tubes. Its displacement is 7,500 tons surfaced and 9,000 submerged. Its dimensions are: length 420 ft; 35 beam ft; and draught 33 ft. The complement is 135 officers and men, alternating between two crews. The diving depth is an excess of 980 feet. Because

9

10

of the long construction period, the submarines have many variations in equipment fits and design. (ECP Armees)

11. The 'Le Redoubtable' class ballistic missile submarine *L'Indomptable* (S 613) pictured while under construction at Cherbourg. As with *Le Tonnant* (S 614), this boat has a metallic reactor core instead of the oxide cores of the earlier boats. (DCAN Cherbourg)

12. The 'Le Redoutable' class submarine *Le Tonnant* seen being launched on 17 September 1977. L'Inflexible (S 615), the sixth boat of the class, is an intermediate design between the first of this class and the next generation of nuclear-powered ballistic missile submarines. (DCAN Cherbourg)

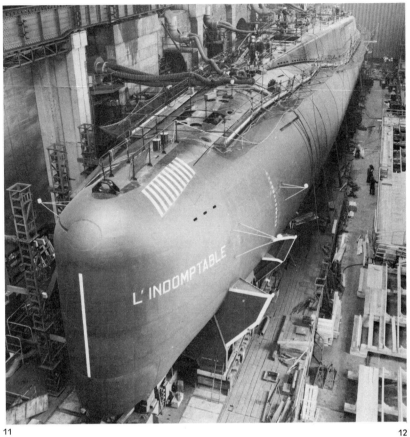

11

12

13. *Agosta* about to be launched on 19 October 1974. This class of conventionally powered attack submarines represents a considerable advance on the earlier 'Narval' class. However, the 'Agostas' have a smaller range, the emphasis being on silent running, and greater diving depth and underwater speed. To aid in achieving this the hull is more streamlined and all deck fittings retract into the outer hull. Three of four boats were launched from 1974 to 1976. (ECP Armees)

14. *Agosta* (S 620) displaces 1,450 tons surfaced and 1,725 tons submerged. The dimensions are: length 222 ft; beam 22ft; and draught 18 ft. Machinery comprises two SEMT-Pielstick 16 PA diesels and electric motors producing 3,600 bhp/4,600 shp. Speed is 12 knots submerged and 20 knots maximum surfaced. The boats are armed with four 550 mm bow torpedo tubes. The sonar fits are DUUA-2, DSUV-2 and DUUX-2. (ECP Armees)

13

14

15. 'Agosta' class attack submarine *La Praya* nearing completion with four other boats under construction. There are four submarines in the class; the other two are *Beveziers* and *Ouessant*. (ECP Armees)

16. *Provence* (S 601), renamed *Rubis*, at the moment of launch on 7th July 1979. The boat underwent trials in 1981 and was completed in 1982. This class of five – three completed and two under construction – nuclear-powered fleet attack submarines resulted from a requirement for a high-performance sous-marine nucleaire de chasse dating from 1964. Armament consists of four 550 mm bow torpedo tubes; 14 torpedoes are carried. (DTCN)

17. An interesting view of *Provence* (now *Rubis*) during launch. The incomplete bow section is for the sonars, which are DSUV-2 passive listening sonars, DUUA-2B active sonars and DUUX-2 or DUUX-5 passive ranging sonars. Several TUUM (UWT) are also fitted. *Rubis* has had a five-month refit, started in 1986. (DTCN)

18. *L'Inflexible* (S 615), commissioned in 1985, is similar to the preceeding 'Le Redoutable' class, but with many improvements in sonars, navigation and the nuclear propulsion system. Weaponry will include twelve torpedoes or SM 39 missiles (from bow tubes), and 16 M-4 missiles each with six TN-70 MIRVed warheads.

17

18

2

BLANDFORD WAR PHOTO-FILES

UNITED KINGDOM

19. HMS *Trump* (S 33), one of eight 'T Conversion' patrol submarines, seen here with the conning tower unstepped in March 1961. The work involved in the reconstruction of these boats from the wartime 'Taciturn' and 'Tabard' groups included lengthening the hull. The underwater speed was 15 knots, over twice the speed previously possible. (Wright and Logan)

20. HMS *Tiptoe* (S 32), a 'T Conversion' submarine seen in 1956, reconstructed, lengthened by 20 ft and with a stepped conning tower. Five of this group were transferred to Israel in the mid-1960s. (Wright and Logan)

19

20

21

21. HMS *Explorer* (S 30) one of two experimental submarines powered by Vickers hydrogen peroxide turbines. The boats were nicknamed 'Exploder' and 'Excruciator' because of numerous mishaps with the perhydrol and there was general relief in the Royal Navy when the boats paid off. Both were broken up during 1964-65. (Wright and Logan)

22. Four 'Stickleback' class midget submarines were ordered in 1951 to replace the old XE-craft. All were launched in 1954-55. *Shrimp*, *Sprat* and *Minnow* were broken up in 1965 and *Stickeback* (X 51), illustrated, was sold to the Swedish Navy but was returned to Britain in 1977 and is now preserved. (Wright and Logan)

23. *Shrimp* (X 52) running on the surface. The speed surfaced was about 6 knots. The 'Sticklebacks' were 53 ft 9 in in length, measured 6 ft in the beam and had a draught of 7 ft 6 in and displaced 32 tons. Two detachable sidecharges could be carried. (Wright and Logan)

24. The 'Stickleback' class were similar in size to the previous X-craft midget submarines, and the space inside the boats was similarly cramped, as this view of the interior of an earlier X-craft shows. (Vickers)

25. This illustration shows HMS *Teredo* (S 38), the 'T' class (third group) submarine, before her modernisation as a 'T Streamlined' patrol submarine. This photograph was taken in May 1957. Compare the appearance of the boat with the photograph of *Teredo* taken in January 1959. (Wright and Logan)

26. HMS *Teredo* (S 38) seen in 1959 as a 'T Streamlined' patrol submarine, with a streamlined casing and fin and the deck guns removed. Five boats underwent this modernisation, which was on similar lines to the 'T Conversion'. All boats were broken up between 1965 and 1970. (Wright and Logan)

27. HMS *Aurochs* (S 62) was the only unmodernised 'A' class boat. This illustration shows her in April 1963 with the external torpedo tubes removed. There were 16 boats in this class, launched in 1945-47. *Aurochs* was broken up in 1967, but other boats remained in service until the early 1970s while *Alliance*

was still service in the early 1980s. (Wright and Logan)

28. The modernised 'A' class patrol submarine HMS *Andrew* (S 63), streamlined but with a 4-in deck gun, seen off Portsmouth in April 1969. (Wright and Logan)

26

27

28

29. HMS *Alliance* (S 67), as with the other 'A' class modernisations, was streamlined on the same lines as the 'T Conversions'. Seen here in September 1967, she has no deck gun, in keeping with most of the class. She was armed with six 21-in torpedo tubes and carried 18 torpedoes or 18 Mark 2 mines. She displaced 1,443 tons when surfaced and was 282 ft in length. (Wright and Logan)

30. HMS *Astute* (S 47), a modernised 'A' class patrol submarine, seen entering Aden Harbour in December 1965 after a tour of duty east of Suez for exercises with ships of the Indian Navy. This tour also included a CENTO exercise in which British, American and Iranian warships took part. (Royal Navy)

29

30

31. HMS *Aeneas* (S 72) was lent to Vickers for trials with the submarine launched anti-aircraft missile (SLAM) before being broken up in 1972. The system, capable of functioning from periscope depth, can be seen mounted on a retractable mast in the forward section of the conning tower with a six-Blowpipe cluster around the TV guidance camera. The system was not adopted. All other 'A' boats were scrapped in 1969-72 but *Alliance* (S 67) was preserved as a memorial in 1979. (Royal Navy)

32. HMS *Porpoise* (S 01), name ship of a class of diesel-electric patrol submarines. This class were the first post-war submarines, apart form the 'Explorer' experimental boats, and many design features resulted from experience gained from trials with the war reparation U-boats. Built between 1955 and 1961 they were a successful class, quiet and therefore difficult to detect. Except for *Sealion* (S 07) and *Walrus* (S 08), they only went out of service in the early 1980s because of the cut-backs imposed on the Royal Navy by the 1975 Defence Review. Another factor was the demands they made on manpower needed to operate the strategic submarines. (Royal Navy)

33. A stern view of HMS *Sealion* (S 07) taken in June 1965. Surface displacement was 1,975 tons and the dimensions were: length 290 ft 3 in; beam 26 ft 6 in; draught 18 ft 3 in. The crew totalled 71 officers and men. (Royal Navy)

34. The coxswain of the 'Porpoise' class submarine HMS *Cachalot* (S 06) on watch at the

32

34

33

after hydroplane controls while the boat is submerged. (Royal Navy)

35. The weapons team aboard HMS *Cachalot* pose for the camera after loading the torpedo tube. 'Porpoise' class boats had six 21-in torpedo tubes forward and two aft, and carried 30 torpedoes. (Royal Navy)

36. HMS *Otter* (S 15), one of the 'Oberon' class patrol boats. Fourteen boats were built for the Royal Navy between 1957 and 1967 and 13 remain in service, *Onyx* (S 21) having been transferred to Canada in 1963. The 'Oberons' were similar in appearance to the 'Porpoise'

class but incorporated improvements which enable greater efficiency, including diving depth and quietness. They are earmarked for disposal when Type 2400 comes into service. (Royal Navy)

35

36

37. HMS *Oberon* (S 09) entering the Grand Harbour, Malta, in June 1973. HMS *St Angelo* is on the port beam. The armament for the 'Oberons' was originally the same as in the 'Porpoise' class, but was altered for Mark 24 Mod 1 torpedoes. The dimensions and machinery details are as for the 'Porpoises'. (Royal Navy)

38. HMS *Opossum* (S 19) making her way through pack ice during Arctic trials (Exercise 'Portent') in March 1965. Note the protective frame over the sonar dome and the large pieces of ice on the deck casing above the forward hydroplanes. (Royal Navy)

39. Crew members at the controls of HMS *Odin* (S 10). (Royal Navy)

37

38

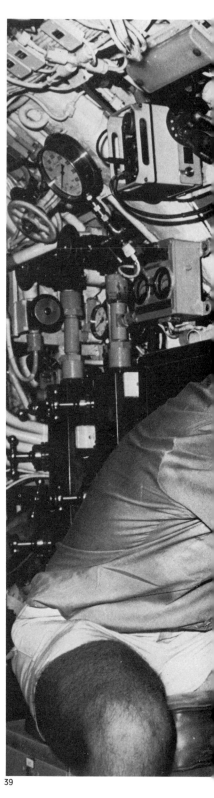

39

40. The engine room of an 'Oberon' class submarine looking aft. The diesel generators supply power to the batteries and electric motors which enable the boat to make up to 12 knots when snorting. (Vickers)

41. Britain's first nuclear-powered submarine was the 3,500-ton HMS *Dreadnought* (S 101) built by Vickers-Armstrong at Barrow in 1959-63. She was earmarked for disposal in 1982. Delays with the land-based Dounreay reactor delayed the nuclear submarine programme so an S5W reactor was obtained from the US Navy, which was constructed by Rolls-Royce. *Dreadnought* was fitted with Types 2001, 2007 and 2019 sonars and had six 21-in torpedo tubes. Twenty-four torpedoes were carried. The boat is seen leaving Faslane. (Royal Navy)

42. The plotting position aboard the attack submarine HMS *Dreadnought*. (Royal Navy)

43. HMS *Dreadnought* rescues 35 seamen from the 7,000-ton freighter *Carnation* after a collision with the 20,000-ton tanker *Anson* in the Malacca Straits in July 1973. The photograph was taken from a helicopter from HMS *Tiger* (C 20). (Royal Navy)

44. HMS *Dreadnought* photographed at the North Pole shortly after her fin broke through the ice. (Royal Navy)

45. HMS *Valiant* (S 102), the 4,000-ton lead boat of a class of nuclear-powered attack submarines. She is powered by a British pressurised water-cooled reactor, developed at the Admiralty Reactor Test Establishment at Dounreay. Her speed submerged is 20 knots and she can make 28 knots surfaced. There are five boats in the class, which is officially divided into two classes 'Valiant' (*Valiant* (S 102), *Warspite* (S 103)) and 'Churchill' (*Churchill* (S 46), *Conqueror* (S 48), *Courageous* (S 50)). (Royal Navy)

46. HMS *Churchill* (S 46) at Faslane. This class of nuclear-powered attack submarines was constructed between 1962 and 1970 and the last boat was commissioned in November 1971. (Royal Navy)

47. HMS *Resolution* (S 22), lead ship of a four-boat class of ballistic missile submarines, leaving Faslane in April 1977. A fifth boat, to be named *Ramillies*, was cancelled in 1964. The 7,500-ton 'Resolution' boats are similar in many respects to the US 'Lafayette' class and are armed with missiles, torpedo tubes and associated fire control systems of US origin. However, British

equipment and machinery is installed. Dimensions are: length 425 ft; beam 33 ft; and, draught 30 ft. (Royal Navy)

48. HMS *Courageous* (S 50) being launched at Barrow on 16 October 1971. The original sonar fit included Tyes 2001, 2007, 183, 197 and 2014. *Courageous* is the only boat in this group to be

refitted with the Typed 2020 long-range passive sonar. (Vickers)

49. Loading a Tigerfish anti-submarine torpedo aboard HMS *Conqueror* (S 48). There are six 21-in torpedo tubes forward and 26 reloads are carried. Mark 24 torpedoes have replaced the earlier Marks 8 and 23. All boats will be fitted

47

48

49

with Sub-Harpoon on refit. *Conqueror* sank the Argentinian cruiser *General Belgrano* on 2 May 1982 with a salvo of two Mark 8 torpedoes during the 1982 Falklands War. (Royal Navy)

50. The ballistic missile compartment of HMS *Resolution* (S 22), showing a crew member carrying out checks at the integrated monitoring panel. A row of Polaris missile launch tubes can be seen on the right, starting with tube three, the inspection door of which is clearly visible. Sixteen Polaris A3TK are carried, each having three MIRV warheads at 60 kilotons each. The new Chevaline warheads are fitted in the missiles on *Resolution, Repulse* (S 23) and *Renown* (S 26) but not in *Revenge* (S 27). (Royal Navy)

51. The torpedo stowage compartment aboard HMS *Resolution* (S 22). *Resolution* has six 21-in torpedo tubes. (Royal Navy)

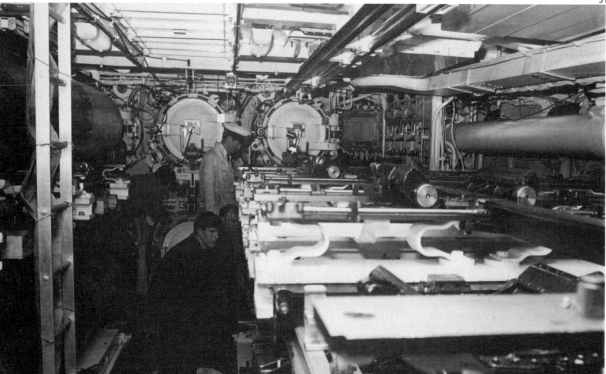

52. Ratings posing for the camera at the diving controls of HMS *Resolution* (S 22) in 1968. The coverings on the monitoring panels are for security purposes. The 'Resolution' boats are powered by a pressurised water-cooled reactor and can make 20 knots surfaced and 25 knots submerged.

53. In May 1979 the Royal Navy and the US Navy co-operated in a simulated 'Subsunk' exercise. During the exercise the deep submergence rescue vehicle *Avalon* was flown from San Diego to Glasgow, and from there went by road to the Clyde Supmarine Base where she was loaded onto the after casing of HMS *Repulse* (S 23). The submarine then sailed to the scene of the 'accident' and *Avalon* was released to search for the 'sunken' submarine, HMS *Odin* (S 10). Using sonar, *Avalon* located *Odin* and attached herself over the escape hatch. The crew was then transferred to *Repulse*. This was the first time that men were transferred between two submarines underwater. (Royal Navy)

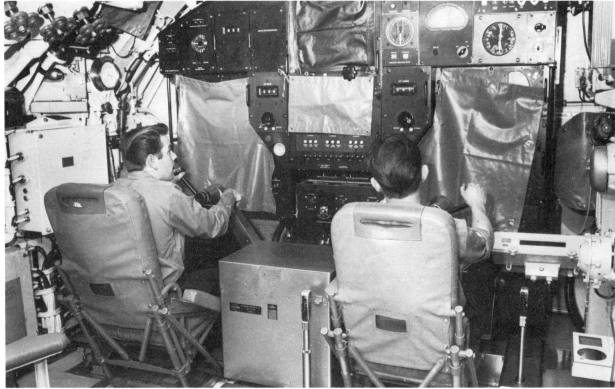

52

53

54. Submarine 'survivors' inside the DSRV *Avalon* being transferred back to HMS *Repulse* (S 23) from the 'sunken' HMS *Odin* (S 10). For details of DSRVs see under United States of America. (Royal Navy)

55. HMS *Swiftsure* (S 126) name ship of a class of nuclear attack submarines, is powered by a pressurised water-cooled reactor. She has a speed of 20 knots surfaced and more than 30 knots submerged. Twenty-five Tigerfish torpedoes are carried and Sub-Harpoon is being installed. (Royal Navy)

56. The 'Swiftsure' class (six boats) are a faster and deeper diving version of the 'Valiants', with a fuller hull-form and one less bow torpedo tube. As can be seen, the diameter of the hull is maintained for a much greater length than in previous classes. *Sovereign* (S 108) is illustrated. (Vickers)

57. HMS *Superb* (S 109) being launched at Barrow on 30 November 1974. 'Swiftsure' class boats displace 4,200 tons surfaced and 4,500 tons submerged. Dimensions are: length 272 ft; beam 32 ft 4 in; and draught 27 ft. (Vickers)

58. HMS *Turbulent* (S 114) second of the 'Trafalgar' class of nuclear-powered attack submarines. Three boats have been commissioned and the rest are either building or fitting out. Displacement is approximately 4,000 tons and the dimensions are: length 28 ft; beam 32 ft; and draught 29 ft 9 in. Sub-Harpoon is carried together with torpedoes

56

57

and mines. These boats resemble the 'Swiftsure' class, but are designed to be quieter. Anechoic tiling on the pressure hull and other surfaces and a pump jet instead of a propeller aid in noise reduction. (Royal Navy)

59. HMS *Trafalgar* (S 113) the first of an improved class of Fleet submarines, was ordered in July 1977, laid down in 1978, launched in 1981 and commissioned on 27 May 1983. (Royal Navy)

60. An artist's impression of a 'Vanguard' class nuclear-powered ballistic missile submarine,

the first member of this four-boat class was laid down in 1986 and is expected to be commissioned in 1991. At first it was decided to purchase the Trident C4 system to replace the Polaris weapons, but it is now intended to equip this class with the Trident D5 system, which has 14 MIRV warheads per missile as opposed to the C4's eight. (Royal Navy)

58

59

60

61. HMS *Upholder* (S 40), the first of a class of Type 2400 diesel-electric patrol submarines being launched at Barrow in December 1986. The Type 2400 is based on a British nuclear design, incorporating a French Type 2046 towed array sonar. Weaponry will include Spearfish wire-guided torpedoes and Sub-Harpoon missiles. (VSEL).

3

BLANDFORD WAR
PHOTO-FILES

UNITED STATES
OF AMERICA

62. The wartime-built 'Gato' class submarine USS *Barb* (SS 220) underwent the 'GUPPY IB Fleet Snorkel' modernisation in 1953-54, which was intended to provide fleet submarines with a snorkel and other modernisations. Some boats retained their deck guns for a short time. *Barb* was transferred to Italy in 1954 and was active until 1973. (US Navy)

63. The 'Tench' class boat USS *Guavina* (SS 362) was converted to perform as a submarine oiler (SSO) in 1950, when the 1930s concept of refuelling seaplanes at forward locations was revived. Apart from her trials with seaplanes, she also refueled USS *Dogfish* (SS 350) underwater in the only operation of its kind by any navy. Used as a training boat until 1967,

she was expended as a target. (Wright and Logan)

64. For 20 years after the war the backbone of the US submarine force was comprised of the best of the wartime 'Gato' class, many of which had undergone rebuilding in one or other of the post-war modernisation programmes.

62

63

64

Some, like USS *Cavalla* (AGSS 244) were given AGSS (research and auxiliary submarine) designations as an administrative measure so that they would not be charged against the US Navy's attack submarine force levels. USS *Cavalla* was built in 1943 and remained active until 1968 and has been preserved as a memorial since 1969. (US Navy)

65. USS *Blenny* (SS 324) was modernised in 1951 in the 'GUPPY 1A' programme. The GUPPY programme was a scheme to improve the underwater performance of fleet submarines by streamlining the hulls by removing the deck guns, rounding the bows and altering conning towers. About 50 conversions were carried out ; some remained in service in the 1970s. (US Navy)

66. A starboard quarter bow view of USS *Razorback* (SS 394), a 'Balao' class GUPPY IIA conversion (1954-70). Transferred to Turkey in 1970 and renamed *Murat Reis*. The four main GUPPY conversions were IA, II, IIA and III, with several minor configurations in between. (US Navy)

65

66

67. The 'Balao' class submarine USS *Greenfinch* (SS 351) was a 1948 GUPPY II conversion and was modernised to GUPPY III standard in 1961. She was transferred to Brazil in 1973 and was renamed *Amazonas*. (Wright and Logan)

68. The 'Tench' class radar picket USS *Requin* (SS 481), the first submarine modified as an SSR boat was active until 1971, and is now preserved as a memorial. Ten boats were converted to radar pickets under the three phases of the 'Mirgraine' programme and equipped with air-search radars. They were intended to scour ahead of the fleet and guide air attacks on enemy aircraft. Advances in shipboard and aircraft radar soon made the SSR concept obsolete. (Wright and Logan)

69. A starboard view of USS *Sailfish* (SS 572) under way. This boat, together with *Salmon* (SS 573), was completed in 1956. They were built to supplement the ten submarines converted to

radar pickets. Their speed was too low for them to keep up with a carrier task force and they were reclassified as attack submarines in March 1961. Both were taken out of service in 1977 and 1978. (US Navy)

70. USS *Salmon* (SS 573) after reclassification from a radar picket to an attack submarine in 1961. Both boats were later given FRAM refits. (US Navy)

71. USS *Tigrone* (AGSS 419) was a 'Tench' class boat converted as a research platform for the US Naval Underwater Sound Laboratory. There is a test installation abaft the conning tower and the cumbersome bow structure houses experimental sound equipment. *Tigrone* was decommissioned and used as a target in 1975. (Wright and Logan)

69

70

71

72. USS *Barracuda* (SST 3),an ex-'K' class attack submarine. Three boats of this small diesel-powered class was built between 1949 and 1952 specifically for the ASW role. These hunter-killer boats were the smallest US submarines built in over 30 years, having a displacement of 765 tons surfaced and a length of 196 ft. The intention was that they would sink enemy submarines as they left their bases, but they were withdrawn from the SSK role in 1959. The large bow structure houses an AN/BQR-4 passive array sonar derived from the German Type XXI's GHG sonar. (US Navy)

73. USS *Tang* (SS 563) operating off Pearl Harbor. The 'Tang' class of six boats were regarded as a US version of the Soviet 'Whiskey' class, the design assimilating many aspects of the German Type XXI. Its displacement was 1,560 tons surfaced and its length was 269 ft. The first four boats had newly-designed compact radial diesel engines – known as 'Pancake' diesels – which caused considerable problems. (US Navy)

72

73

74

74. USS *Darter* (SS 576) at speed during her sea trials in 1956. This boat was an improved version of the 'Tang' class with a greater surface speed, 19.5 knots, and an increased diving depth. Two other hulls intended for completion as 'Darter' class boats were instead completed as strategic missile submarines. (US Navy)

75. USS *Mackerel* (SST 1), one of two 303 ton target submarines, originally ordered as AGSS 570 and numbered T1. The other vessel in the class was USS *Marlin* (SST 2). Both were deactivated on 31 January 1973. (US Navy)

76. The design of the midget submarine X 1 was influenced by the British World War Two X-

Craft, one of which was taken to the United States for study. Launched in 1955, this was the only US boat to use a hydrogen peroxide propulsion plant. An internal explosion broke her in three in February 1958. She was then rebuilt and was used as a test boat between 1960 and 1973, then stricken from the active list. She displaced 31 tons surfaced. (US Navy)

75

76

77. USS *Nautilus* (SSN 571) was the world's first nuclear-powered warship. She and *Seawolf* (SSN 575) were the prototypes for the US nuclear submarine programme. *Nautilus* was powered by an S2W reactor and could make about 23 knots submerged. She displaced 3,533 tons surfaced and 4,092 tons submerged. Her length was 323 ft 9 in, beam 27 ft 8 in and draught 21 ft 9 in. Armament consisted of six 21 in bow torpedo tubes. *Nautilus* is shown on her initial sea trials in June 1955. She was preserved as a museum ship in 1982.

78. USS *Nautilus* (SSN 571) had a remarkable first two years of operations in which she established several records for underwater speed and endurance until her first uranium fuel core replacement in April 1957. Her first reactor core drove her for 65,562 miles, her second for 91,324 and her third for about 150,000 miles. *Nautilus* made initial probes under the arctic ice in 1957. In 1958, she succeeded in penetrating the ice between Alaska and Siberia. On 3 August 1958, she

77

crossed the North Pole, under the ice, then moved south to enter the open Atlantic between Greenland and Iceland. The illustration shows the watch crew in the control room under the ice cap. (US Navy)

79. USS *Seawolf* (SSN 575), commissioned in 1957, passes under the Golden Gate. At first she

had an S2G sodium-cooled reactor but because of operational problems this was replaced by an S2Wa model. *Seawolf* has been engaged mainly in research work since 1969. (US Navy)

80. USS *Skate* (SSN 578) under way off Long Island on her first sea voyage in 1957. This, the world's third nuclear-powered submarine, was

the first production model of the four-boat 'Skate' class. Similar in design to the *Nautilus* but considerably smaller, this class displaced 2,550 tons surfaced and had a length of 267 ft 8 in. The reactor plants developed under the 'Skate' programme, S3W and S4W, were an improvement on earlier types. Three boats remain in service. (US Navy)

79

80

81. USS *Albacore* (AGCS 569), with her revolutionary 'tear drop' hull design, was capable of approximately 33 knots submerged. This successful configuration was to be the basis for all subsequent US nuclear submarine hull designs. This 1,500-ton, 210-ft boat was extensively modified during her operational life. The illustration shows her with the original conventional stern surfaces, which were replaced in 1961 with X-form planes. *Albacore* was laid up in reserve in 1972. One other experimental submarine, USS *Dolphin* (AGCS 555), a deep-diving boat, is still in use. (US Navy)

82. USS *Barbel* (SS 580) slipping down the ways during her launching ceremony at Portsmouth Naval Shipyard, New Hampshire, on 19 July 1958. The three boats of the 'Barbel' class were the last US diesel-electric submarines to be built, and the streamlined 'tear-drop' hull form of USS *Albacore* was adopted to enable short bursts of high underwater speed. (US Navy)

81

82

83. As built USS *Barbel* (SS 580) and the other two boats had conventional bow diving planes, as can be seen in the launching photograph, but they were modified with planes on the sail as in this illustration. All controls were centralised in an 'attack centre' to increase efficiency. This arrangement has been adopted for subsequent US sumbarmines. (US Navy)

84. The 'Barbel' class displaced 2,146 tons surfaced and 2,639 tons submerged. Dimensions are: length 219 ft 2 in; beam 29; and draught 20 ft 8 in. Power is supplied by three FM diesels and one Westinghouse electric motor. Armament consists of six 21-in bow torpedo tubes. The Sonar is BOS-4. All three boats are in service. (US Navy)

83

84

85. Six 'Skipjack' class attack submarines were laid down, launched and completed between 1956 and 1961. *Skipjack* (SSN 585) and four other boats are in service: *Scorpion* (SS 589) was lost southwest of the Azores in May 1968. Armament consists of six 21-in bow torpedo tubes, 24 torpedoes are carried. The illustration shows *Skipjack* executing a sharp turn at speed during her initial sea trials.

86. USS *Snook* (SSN 592) the last of the 'Shipjack' class to be completed. This class were the first to use the S5W reactor and are reported to be capable of approximtely 30 knots submerged. They were the fastest US Navy submarines until the 'Los Angeles' boats. They displace 3,070 tons surfaced and 3,500 tons submerged. Their dimensions are: length 251 ft 9 in; beam 31 ft 8 in; and draught 25 ft 3 in. (US Navy)

87. The nuclear-powered attack submarine USS *Tuilibee* (SSN 597) was the result of an attempt

85

86

87

to build as small a nuclear-powered submarine as possible for ASW. The result was an underpowered boat, moving at approximately 15 knots when submerged. The reactor used was an S2C. She displaced 2,316 tons surfaced and was 272 ft 10 in long. Originally a BQQ-2 sonar was fitted but she was later fitted with three PUFFS hydrophones in three fins along the top of the hull for BQG-4 passive sonar. These have now been removed. BQS-12 active and BQR-7 passive sonar now complement the BQG-4. (Us Navy)

88. A bow view of USS *Thresher* (SSN 593) taken on 24 July 1961. *Thresher*, the first of the 'Thresher/Permit' class was lost during diving trials on 10 April 1963. She was designed to dive deeper and operate more quietly than previous SSNs, being constructed from improved HY-80 steel, sound-isolated machinery and having other special characteristics. (US Navy)

89. USS *Plunger* (SSN 595) under way off the coast of Oahu, Hawaii. Including *Thresher* this group numbered eleven boats. However, the 'Sturgeon' group was officially a sub-division of the 'Permit/Sturgeon' class, which together form the largest class of submarines built by the USA since World War Two. These boats were originally intended for ASW and can carry ASW torpedoes, nuclear-tipped torpedoes, anti-ship torpedoes, or SUBROC, Harpoon and Tomahawk. Weapon capacity, though, is reported to be as low as 20 torpedoes. Mark 117 torpedo fire control systems replaced the Mark 113. They displace 3,705 tons surfaced and measure 278 ft 6 in in length, except for *Jack* (SSN 605) which is 296 ft 9 in. (US Navy)

90. A bow view of USS *Sturgeon* (SSN 637) off Montauk Point, Long Island. The 42 boats in this sub-division of the 'Permit/Sturgeon' class were completed between 1966 and 1975. Only 37 members of the group remain in service. (US Navy)

91. The nuclear-powred 'Sturgeon' class submarine USS *Narwhal* (SSN 671) running surfaced. The S5W reactor produced 15,000 shp, enabling a speed of approximately 26 knots submerged to be reached. Armament details are the same as for the 'Permits' but they are much larger, having a displacement of 4,246 tons surfaced and a length of 292 ft 3 in,

except for *Archerfish* (SSN 678) which is 302 feet. *Narwhal* was a test boat for normal-circulation S5G reactor and is not properly part of the class.

92. USS *General P. Lipscomb* (SSN 685), although officially listed with the 'Sturgeon' class, was a test bed for alternative propulsion systems and

is not, like *Narwhal*, properly part of the group. Used to test a turbo-electric drive, in the search for underwater quietness, but at considerable cost in size, she displaced 5,800 tons and had a length of 365 feet. (General Dynamics)

91

92

93

93. A bow view of the 'Sturgeon' class USS *General P. Lipscomb* running at speed on the surface. These boats are larger than the 'Permit' group and can be readily identified by their taller sail which is 20 ft 6 in above the deck and the much lower position of the diving planes on the sail. The planes rotate to the vertical for surfacing through ice. (US Navy)

94. The 6,00-ton (surfaced) USS *Los Angeles* (SSN 688) nuclear-powered attack submarine is the lead boat of the 'Los Angeles' class of which 33 were in service in early 1987 with 25 either proposed or building. (Newport News)

95. A high oblique port bow view of the 'Los Angeles' class nuclear-powered attack submarine USS *San Francisco* (SSN 711) during sea trials on 15 March 1981. All boats can lay mines, and have SUBROC and Mark 48 ASW torpedoes. Harpoon and Tomahawk missiles will be carried by some members of the class, and 15 vertical-launch tubes are being fitted in the bows of these boats, between the inner and outer hulls. (Newport News)

94

95

96. An aerial bow view of USS *Los Angeles* (SSN 688) under way in the Atlantic. The high displacement in this class is because of the installation of the S6G reactor, which doubled the power available in the 'Sturgeons'. Speed submerged 31 knots; silencing is improved Dimensions are: length 360 ft; beam 33 ft; and draught 32 ft 4 in. (Newport News)

97. A stern view of USS *San Francisco* (SSN 711) under way during sea trials in March 1981. The sensors carried include the BQQ-5 bow sonar and the UKY-7 computer is installed to aid command and control procedures, and eleven boats have the WSC-3 satellite communications transceiver. *San Juan* (SSN 51) and later boats will have the ISM SUBACS (Submarine Advanced Combat System) integrated sonar/weapons control system. (Newport News)

98. The 'Los Angeles' class submarine USS *Honolulu* (SSN 718) seen during her commissioning ceremony on 6 July 1985 with giant leis (Hawaiian for garlands of flowers) decorating the sail. Crewmen stood on deck

96

97

98

USS HONOLULU
SSN-718

under the 'Union Jack', which is the dark blue canton, with the fifty stars, from the national flag. (US Navy)

99. USS *Grayback* (SSG 574) in her guise as a strategic submarine. Only one firing of the Regulus II missile took place and this was from *Grayback*. She could carry four Regulus I or II missiles and had six bow and two stern 21-in torpedo tubes. *Grayback* displaced 2,287 tons surfaced and is 322 ft 4 in in length. Earlier conversion of Fleet boats to strategic submarines included seven other boats, including *Cusk* and *Carbonero*, for the Loon missile programme. (US Navy)

100. USS *Growler* (SSG 577) was purpose-built as a strategic submarine. The Regulus missile programme heralded the era of the strategic strike role for US submarines. However, with the cancellation of the Regulus II programme, all boats earmarked as SSGNs were constructed as 'Thresher' class attack submarines. (US Navy)

99

100

101. USS *Grayback* (LPSS 574) under way in San Francisco Bay in July 1969. *Grayback* and *Growler* (SSG 577) were laid down as sisters to *Darter* but were then lengthened by 50 ft to accommodate two cylindrical hangars for Regulus missiles. Both boats were decommissioned in 1965 when the Regulus programme was halted but *Grayback* was converted to an amphibious transport in 1967. She was reclassified as an attack boat in 1975 and is now in reserve. (US Navy)

102. A close-up of USS *Grayback's* (LPSS 574) 'cargo' hangars, viewed from the bridge looking forward. These former missile hangars have been converted to 'lock out' swimmers and swimmer delivery vehicles. One of the three deck-mounted PUFFS BQG-4 passive sonar domes can be seen forward of the hangar doors. (US Navy)

103. USS *Halibut* (SSGN) was constructed with two enlarged hangars for either two Regulus II or five Regulus I cruise missiles. The hangars

101

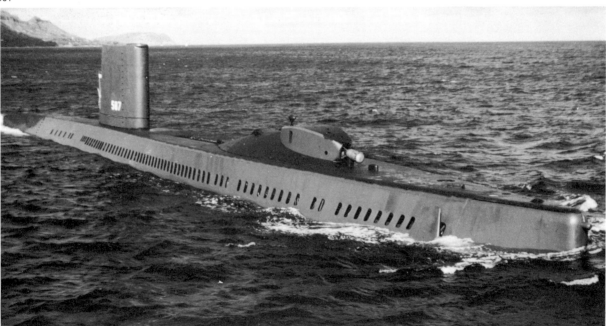

were removed after the Regulus programme ended and she was reclassified as a research submarine from 1965 until 1976 when she was decommissioned. The photograph shows *Halibut* in June 1968. Her displacement was 3,846 tons surfaced and she was 350 ft in length. (US Navy)

104. USS *George Washington* (SSBN 598) lead boat of a class of five fleet ballistic missile submarines under way. She was laid down in 1957, and remained in service as an SSBN until 1981 when she was relegated to SSN status. Sixteen Polaris missiles provided the strategic armament, while six 21-in bow torpedo tubes provided the defensive element. This class was converted from Polaris A-1 to A-3 missiles, but were unable to take on Poseidon and were decommissioned in 1981. (US Navy)

105. USS *Abraham Lincoln* (SSBN 602), a 'George Washington' class submarine, had her missile section removed in 1981, as did *Theodore Roosevelt* (SSBN 600). The other three members of the class had their missile tubes filled with cement and fire control systems removed to comply with the provisions of the SALT Treaty. (US Navy)

106. A series of underwater photographs of a Polaris missile being launched from USS Theodore Roosevelt (SSBN 600). (US Navy)

104

105

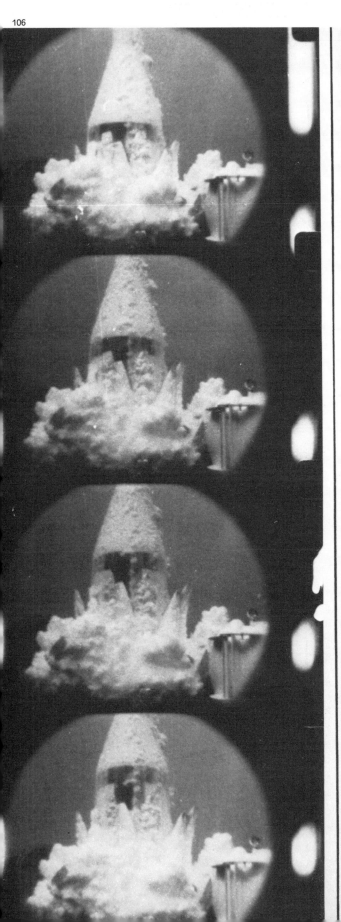

107. Blue and Gold crews of the 'George Washington' class strategic submarine USS *Patrick Henry* (SSBN 599) line up on deck for a change of command ceremony. The submarine is tied up alongside USS proteus (AS 19). (US Navy)

108. The 5,959-ton 'George Washington' class strategic submarine USS *Robert E. Lee* (SSBN 601) seen at the US *Bangor* missile base, Washington state, having America's last Polaris A-3 missile hoisted from her launch tube in 1982. The off-loading marked the end of the US Polaris submarine deployment; the US Navy now deploy larger submarines armed with the longer-range and more powerful Trident Is, the last of which were delivered in January 1986. Fabrication of and testing of Tridents II missiles is now under way. The *Robert E. Lee*, like others of its class, was converted from a fleet ballistic missile submarine (SSBN) to a nuclear fast attack boat or SSN. This class is now decommissioned and in inactive status.

109. USS *Ethan Allen* (SSBN 608). This class consisted of five boats, built between 1959 and 1963, but only two remain in service. These have now been relegated to SSN status because they could not be refitted with the Poseidon missile. All boats were originally armed with Polaris A-2 and later Polaris A-3. Four 21-in bow torpedo tubes are also fitted. The intention to install Tomahawk vertical launchers was abandoned.

108

109

110. A sequence of views of a ZUGM-73A Poseidon missile being fired from the USS *Casimir Pulaski* (SSBN 633) in August 1971. (US Navy)

111. A stern view of USS *Ethan Allen* (SSBN 608). The S5W reactor produces 15,000 shp allowing a speed of approximately 20 knots. Surface displacement is 6,946 tons and the length is 410 ft 5 in. *Sam Houston* (SSBN 609) and *John Marshall* (SSBN 611) were modified as amphibious transports at Puget Sound Naval Shipyard from 1983 to 1985. (US Navy)

112. USS *Lafayette* (SSBN 616) underway off the coast of Norfolk, Virginia. The 'Lafayette' class is an enlarged version of the 'Ethan Allen' class and originally numbered 31 boats; however, the last twelve are generally regarded as a separate class. (US Navy)

110

111

112

113. USS *Henry Clay* (SSBN 625) launching a Polaris missile. The first eight submarines in the 'Lafayette' class were fitted with Polaris A-2 missiles, the next 23 with Polaris A-3. SSBN 620 and SSBN 622-25 were subsequently rearmed with Polaris A-3 in 1968-70. USS *James Madison* (SSBN 627) was the first boat to be converted to carry Poseidon. In 1978-82, twelve of the class were converted to carry Trident I missiles. In order to keep within the SALT agreement limitations, USS *Sam Rayburn* (SSBN 635) had her missile tubes plugged with cement on the commissioning of USS *Alaska* (SSBN 732) early in 1986. (US Navy)

114. The 'Lafayette' class submarine USS *Daniel Boone* (SSBN 629). Patrol endurance is 60 days and a 32-day refit takes place between patrols. Every sixth year each boat has a 16-month overhaul. Of the original 31 boats of this combined 'Benjamin Franklin', 'Lafayette' and 'James Madison' class of ballistic missile submarines, 29 remain in service. (US Navy)

113

114

115. A starboard bow view of the 'Lafayette' class submarine USS *John C. Calhoun* (SSBN 630) under way at speed. The boats are powered by a Westinghouse S5W pressurised water-cooled reactor. Speed is 20 knots surfaced and approximately 30 knots submerged. (US Navy)

116. USS *Stonewell Jackson* (SSBN 634) off Mare Island Naval Shipyard a few months before her commissioning in 1964. The first 'Lafayette' class boat was laid down in 1961 and the last boat, properly a 'Benjamin Franklin' class, was commissioned in 1967. (US Navy)

117. USS *Sam Rayburn* (SSBN 635) is no longer active, her missile tubes being filled with cement to keep the US Navy within the limits of the SALT agreement. The surface displacement of 'Lafayette' boats is 6,650-7,250 tons and submerged displacement is 8,250 tons. Dimensions are: length 425 ft; beam 33 ft; and draught 31 ft. (USAF)

115

116

117

118. 'Lafayette' class submarine USS *Ulysses S. Grant* (SSBN 631) off Apra Harbor, Guam, in January 1969. The commanding officer of the submarine, Commander Raymond E. Engle, is standing by their periscope. (US Navy)

119. USS *Benjamin Franklin* (SSBN 640) off the coast of Oahu, Hawaii. This submarine and eleven subsequent boats are fitted with quieter machinery than earlier 'Lafayette' boats and are regarded as a separate class. (US Navy)

120. The 'Benjamin Franklin' group submarine USS *Kamehameha* (SSBN 642). All fleet ballistic missile submarines have diesel-electric stand-by-machinery, snorts and an outboard auxiliary propeller for emergency use. (US Navy)

121. Polaris A3 missiles being loaded on board the 'Lafayette' class strategic missile submarine USS *Stonewall Jackson* (SSBN 634). (US Navy)

120

122. USS *Ohio* (SSBN 726), the first Trident submarine, under construction on the pier at General Dynamics' Electric Boat Division, Groton, Connecticut, following roll-out from the covered construction hall. Eight boats of the 16,000-ton, 560-ft class have been commissioned, four are building, one is on order and five more are projected. (US Navy)

121

122

123

124

125

124. The 'Ohio' class submarine USS *Michigan* (SSBN 727) under construction. The circle on the upper right is the keel of the USS *Georgia* (SSBN 729). *Ohio* is in the water, and the tent enclosure on the pier is for the keel laying ceremony for the *Georgia* and the christening ceremony for *Ohio*. (US Navy)

125. The commissioning ceremony for the 'Ohio' class Trident submarine USS *Alabama* (SSBN 731) on 25 May 1985. The size of this, the largest US submarine built to date, was vindicated mainly by the 6,000-mile range required for the missiles and the much larger reactor and propulsion system needed to drive the boat. The machinery consists of a General Electric pressurised-water cooled S8G reactor and two geared turbines. Speed is in excess of 20 knots. (General Dynamics)

126. A Trident I (C-4) SLBM being launched from USS *Ohio* (SSBN 726) during a demonstration on a shakedown operation in January 1982. (US Navy)

127. A port bow view of the 'Ohio' class submarine USS *Alabama* (SSBN 731) taken during sea trials in April 1985. This class has 24 tubes for Trident I missiles, which have a range of 4,250 nm and a MIRV capability. The Mark 500 manoeuvering re-entry vehicle (MARV) is under development for Trident I. The Mark 500 is not terminally guided and is intended to evade ABM interceptor missiles. Trident II (D5) will be fitted in SSBN 734 onwards. Mark 5 higher yield re-entry warheads are under development for the D-5. (General Dynamics)

128. USS *Triton* (SSRN 586) was an attempt to solve the low-speed problem of the conventional diesel-electric radar picket submarines by the use of nuclear power. *Triton* had two S4G reactors and could make 27 knots

126

127

surfaced. She was the first US submarine with a three-deck hull. She was laid down in 1959 and completed in 1959. In 1961 she was reclassified as an attack submarine and she was eventually decommissioned in 1969. (US Navy)

129. The 150-ton bathyscaph *Trieste* built by Professor August Piccard, was launched in 1953. The deep submergence vessel was chartered by the US Office of Naval Research in 1957 and purchased in 1958. The illustration shows *Trieste* in 1959 in her original configuration. (US Navy)

130. *Trieste* (DSV 1) wallowing on the surface off the coast of Boston. The small propellers are for underwater manoeuvring and the large radar reflector is intended to be an aid for location on surfacing. A two-man craft capable of diving to a depth of 20,000 ft, bouyancy is supplied by 34,000 gallons of gasoline which is lighter than water. (US Navy)

129

130

131. *Alvin* (DSV 2) and *Turtle* (DSV 3) at the General Dynamics' yard. *Turtle*, the furthest from the camera, can be identified by the large bow observation port. The construction of these DSVs was prompted by the limited horizontal ability of the *Trieste*. (US Navy)

132. *Sea Cliff* (DSV 4) has a diving capability of 5,000 ft, the same as *Alvin* and *Turtle*. *Sea Cliff* was refitted with a titanium pressure sphere to withstand operations at a depth of 20,000 ft. Apart from *NR-1*, all deep submergence vehicles are transported to the site of the operation by ship or submarine. (US Navy)

133. An aerial view of the nuclear-powered submarine USS *Pintado* (SSN 672), with Mystic (DSRV 1) embarked, off the coast of San Diego in March 1977. Previous deep submergence vessels had been for oceanographic and other Navy related deep ocean research but the deep submergence rescue vehicle (DSRV) was

131

132

intended for quick reaction world-wide rescue of sailors trapped on sunken submarines. The white markings on the *Pintado* are intended to assist in recognition during an underwater rendezvous. (US Navy)

134. *Mystic* (DSRV 1) under construction showing the three-sphere pressure conpartment being installed in the fibreglass outer hull. The hemispherical protrusion under the centre sphere is sealed over the hatch of a stricken submarine, permitting crew members to transfer to the DSRV at the same pressure as the submarine. The rescued crewmen would then be transferred to another submarine and the DSRV can then return for a further 24 survivors. (Lockheed)

134

135. *Avalon* (DSRV 2), like her sister *Mystic*, can operate to the maximum survival depths of US submarine pressure hulls. Both DSRVs are fully transportable by air, road, ship and submarine to provide a quick response in the event of a submarine sinking. (US Navy)

136. *NR-1*, the US Navy's nuclear-powered underwater research and ocean engineering vehicle, at the end of her sea trials in 1969. This small submarine is unarmed and is used to recover weapons from the ocean bed and as an aid in the seafloor acoustic monitoring systems programme. (General Dynamics)

135

4

BLANDFORD WAR
PHOTO-FILES

SMALLER NATO
NAVIES

137. The Royal Canadian's Navy's 'Oberon' type submarine *Onondaga* (SS 73) seen in June 1967. There are two other vessels in this class, *Ojibwa* (SS 72) (ex-Oynx) and *Okanagan* (SS 74). All boats were built at Chatham Dockyard and were launched between 1964 and 1966. They are similar to the British 'Oberon' class but have Mark 37-C ASW torpedoes instead of anti-ship weapons. Following a Submarine Operational Update Programme (SOUP), begun in 1980, all boats have received new sonar arrangements and a new fire control system. US Mark 8 torpedoes and Sub-Harpoon missiles will be embarked. The RCN had a US 'Balao' class and a US 'Tench' class submarine in service from 1961 and 1968 respectively. The vessels were returned to the US in 1969 and 1974. (Wright and Logan)

138. *Wilhelm Bauer* (Y 888), an ex-Type XXI submarine, was used for experimental purposes after a total refit in 1960. She was decommissioned in 1982.

137

138

139. Type 205 coastal submarine *U-10* (S 189). There were originally eleven boats in this class but only six remain in service *U-1(ii)* (S 180), *U-2(ii)* (S 181) and *U-9* to *U-12* (S 188-191). With the exception of *U-2(ii)*, all boats in this class were to be of the Type 201 design. However, because of corrosive defects in the Type 201s, *U-4* to *U-8* were sheathed in tin, causing severe operational problems. Construction of *U-9* to *U-12* was postponed until a special non-magnetic metal was developed. (Marineamt)

140. *U-1(ii)* – in mid-1962 the appearance of structural weakness, which rapidly increased, led to the decommissioning of the Type 210s *U-1* and *U-2*. They were later rebuilt as Type 205s. Their displacement is 419 tons surfaced and 455 tons submerged. Unlike the Type 201, the Type 205 has a totally enclosed conning tower. They are armed with eight torpedoes but can carry 16 mines instead.

141. An usual view of Type 206 boats U-23 (S 172) and *U-24* (S 173) during transit after construction. Germany's first class of operational submarine after the war was the ex-Type XXIII boats named *Hai* (ex-*U-2365*) and *Hect* (ex-*U-2367*). However, the first boat to be commissioned was the ex-Type XXI *Wilhelm* *Bauer* (ex-U-2540), an experimental submarine which was never considered as an operational unit.

142. Port, starboard, stern and bow views of *U-29* (S 178) a Type 206 patrol submarine. There are 18 boats in this class, designed in 1964-65 by IKL and launched from 1971 to 1974. They were built variously by Howaldtswerke in Kiel and RNSW in Emden. The Type 206 is a larger development of the Type 205. They benefit from improvements in metallurgy which were the product of research carried out to overcome the corrosion problem which beset that class – uniquely, the hulls are constructed from high-tensile non-magnetic steel.

141

142

143. The interior arrangement of the Type 206 is similar to that of the Type 201 and Type 205. The radar is a Calypso navigation/attack set, as in the Type 205, and the sonar is AN410A4, AN5039A1 and DBQS-21D. Twelve boats of this class will be modernised from 1988 to 1991, which will include new Krupp Atlas DBQS-21D sonar and an improved weapons control system for the Seal 3 torpedoes. New periscopes and mast and other modifications will also be part of the modernisation programme. (Bundesministerium)

144. The Federal Republic of Germany has developed small conventional coastal patrol submarines in part because it was not allowed to build larger boats after the war, and partly because the main operational areas of its navy are in shallow waters – the Baltic and the North Sea – where large submarines cannot operate satisfactorily. The development of these small boats has brought Germany many orders from abroad, and experiments are in progress with air-independent propulsion systems which will enable a submarine to remain submerged without having to snort or surface. This system is intended for a new Type 208 submarine to be produced in the 1990s. The boat illustrated is U-14 (S 193), a Type 206, clearly showing the main visual difference from the earlier Type 201s and 205s – the rounded bow and sonar dome. (Bundesministerium)

145. The Type 206 couples high underwater manoeuvrability with less underwater noise than earlier types. Submerged range is reported to be 200 nautical miles at 5 knots.

144

145

146

The illustration shows *U-24* (S 173) making way in heavy weather (Marineamt)

146. Eight Type 209 'Glavkos' class submarines were built for Greece by Howalkswerke between 1968 and 1980, in two groups. The first four boats proved cramped so the length of the second group was increased to 183 ft 5 in from 178 ft 6 in. This class has all but replaced the ex-US 'Gato', 'Balao' and 'Tench' classes transferred after World War Two.

147. *U-25* (S 174). Type 206s displace 456 tons when surfaced and 500 tons when submerged. The dimensions are: length 159 ft 6 in; beam 15 ft; and draught 14 ft. Machinery is the same as in the Type 201, a single-shaft electric drive consisting of Mercedes Benz diesels plus one electric motor. Armament consists of eight 533 mm torpedo tubes (16 torpedoes) and 24 mines which can be carried in a pair of external GRP containers. (Bundesministerium)

148. The 'Delfinen' class was the first Danish-design since World War Two. Four boats were built with US 'offshore' funds between 1954 and 1961. They displace 595 tons surfaced and are 178 ft 10 in long. Two boats remain, *Springeren* (S 329) (illustrated) and *Spaekhuggeren* (S 327). (Wright and Logan)

149. The two boats of the 'Narhvalen' class were constructed at the Royal Dockyard in Copenhagen between 1965 and 1970. The class is a modified version of the Improved Type 205 design. These 370-ton boats are capable of 12 knots surfaced and 17 knots submerged. *Nordkaperen* (S 321) is illustrated.

150. Launching a 'Nazario Sauro' class submarine at Itralcantieri's Monfalcone yard. The first pair of this six boat-class were authorised in 1972 and came into service in 1980, with the second pair being laid down in 1979-80 and entering service in 1982. The reasons for the delay between the two pairs were budgetary and technical problems.

148

149

151. *Attilio Bagnolini* (S505), one of the four 'Toti' class boats. These were the first indigenous submarines to be built in Italy after the war and are classed as hunter-killers. The boats are small – displacement 535 tons surfaced; length 151 ft 8 in – but highly manoeuvrable, with a surface speed of 20 knots. Armament consists of four 533 mm bow torpedo tubes with possibly only two reloads. Italy also has two ex-US Navy 'Tang' boats in service.

152. *Nazario Sauro* (S 518) lead boat of the class photographed in May 1980 at the Third Italian Naval Exhibition. The other vessels in the illustration are the guided missile hydrofoil *Sparviero* (P 420) and the flight deck of the survey vessel *Ammiraglio Magnaghi* (A5303). The fifth boat of the 'Sauro' class was launched at the Fincantieri yard in December 1986. She and the sixth boat incorporate a number of internal improvements, including longer torpedo tubes to enable the Sub-Harpoon to be fired. (S. Petani/P. Marsan)

151

152

153

153. A stern view of a 'Nazario Sauro' class submarine being launched. The seven-bladed propeller, designed to reduce cavitation and, therefore, noise and the possibility of detection, is driven by three diesels, and there is one electric motor. Speed is 12 knots submerged and 20 knots surfaced. Range is estimated at 7,000 nm. (Italcantieri)

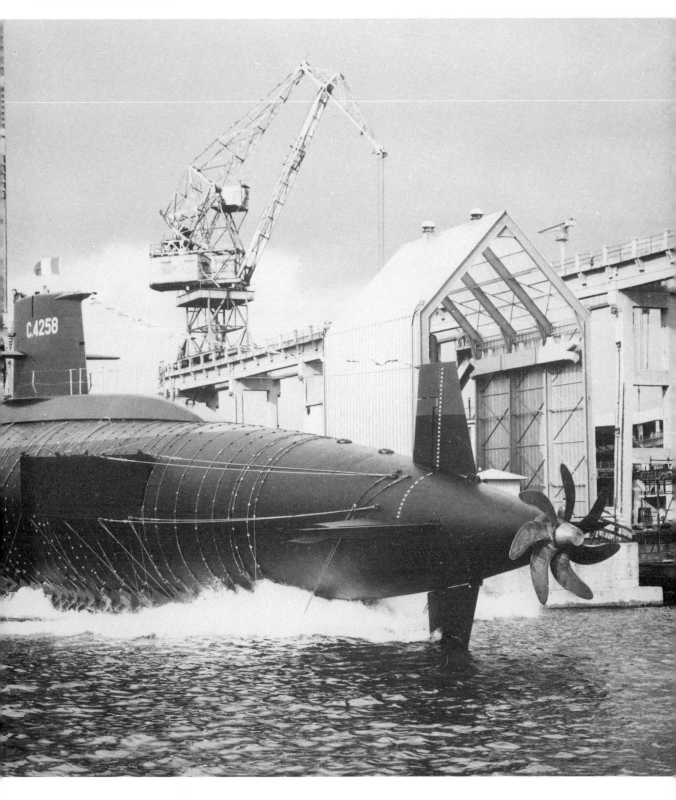

154. *Nazario Sauro* (S 518) has six 533 mm torpedo tubes and can carry six reload torpedoes. The weapons system is an SISU-1 which can tack four targets simiultaneously. The latest boat in the improved class, *Salvatore Pelosi* (S 522) and her sister *Giuliano Prini* (S 523), will have an updated version of the Whitehead and USEA IPD70 integrated system.

Ferranti is supplying equipment to refit the steering control systems in the earliest boats. Displacement: 1,456 tons surfaced, 1,641 tons submerged. Dimensions: length 209 ft 7 in; beam 22 ft 5 in; draught 18 ft 9 in.

155. Four 'Dolfijn'/'Potvis' class submarines were commissioned in 1949. Two were laid

down in 1954 and completed in 1960-61, but further construction was halted while the possibility of nuclear propulsion was investigated. As the use of nuclear reactors would have resulted in a complex redesigning of the remaining boats, with resultant prohibitive costs, it was decided to reinstate the order for the remaining two boats. These

154

were completed in 1965-66 with modifications. The boat illustrated is *Zeehond*, of the first pair. (Wright and Logan)

156. *Potvis* (S 804), of the second pair of 'Dolfijn' class submarines. of which only three are still in service. It displaces 1,494 tons surfaced and measures 261 feet in length. Two MAN diesels and two electric motors produce 3,100 bhp/4,400 hp, giving a speed of 14.5 knots submerged and 17 knots surfaced. There are four bow and four stern torpedo tubes. (Wright and Johnson)

157. Two 'Walrus' class attack-submarines have been launched and two more are to be built. Intended to replace the 'Potvis' and 'Dolfijn' boats, they will have higher underwater speed and manoeuvrability and a deeper diving capability. A fifth boat is planned to be laid down in the 1990s when the second pair are completed.

156

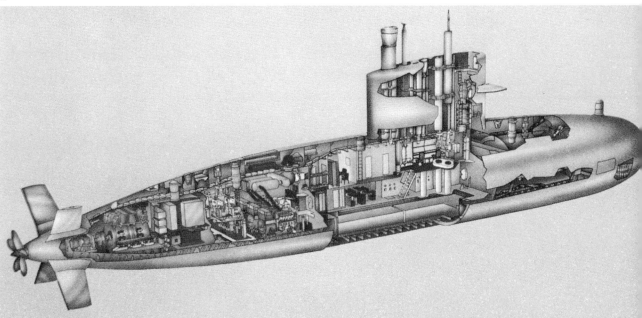

158. The 'Zwaardvis' class submarine were constructed by Rotterdamse Droogdok Mij between 1966 and 1972, and are similar to the US 'Barbel' class, but have 'Albacore' type hulls for a higher speed than the triple-hulled 'Dolfijn' class. *Tijgerhaai* (S 807) is illustrated.

159. The ex-German Type VIIC submarine *U-1202* was acquired by Norway from Great Britain in 1950 and named *Kinn* (S 308). The boat remained in service until 1961. Two other similar boats were taken out of service in 1963 and 1964. (Wright and Logan)

160. *Albacora* (S 163),one of four Portuguese French 'Daphne' type submarines, which were ordered in 1964 and came into service between 1967 and 1969. *Cachalote* (S 165) was transferred to Pakistan in 1975, leaving *Albacora*, *Baraacuda* (S 164) and *Delfim* (S 166) still in service. These boats replaced the three

158

159

160

161

ex-British 'S' class patrol submarines which were acquired in 1948 and deactivited in 1967-69. (Wright and Logan)

161. Under the 1959 five-year programme, Norway and the US shared the cost of building the 15 'Kobben' class submarines. This class is an improved version of the Type 207, but with greater diving depth. The displacement is 370 tons surfaced. Its dimensions are: length 149 ft, beam 15 ft and draught 14 ft. *Skolpen* (S 306) is illustrated.

162. A Sea King helicopter from the aircraft carrier HMS *Ark Royal* (R 09) evacuates a casualty from the Portuguese patrol submarine *Barracuda* (S 164) on 1 October 1976. *Ark Royal* was in Lisbon harbour at the time, following Exercise 'Teamwork' when she was requested to assist. The casevac was successfully executed in fairly rough seas 75 miles southwest of Lisbon. See the French section for details of the 'Daphne' class. (Royal Navy)

163. Spain has four 'S 60' submarines which are based on the French 'Daphne' class. These boats were built by Bazian at Cartagena between 1968 and 1975, and have since undergone extensive modernisation, including updating the fire control and torpedo handling system and the sonar fit. *Delfin* (S 61) is illustrated. (Dr Giorgio Arra)

162

163

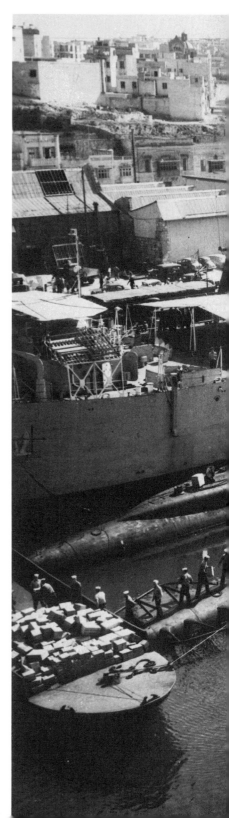

164. The nearest boat is *Canakkale* (S-333), which was active as USS Bumper (SS 333) until 1950. She underwent Fleet Snorkel conversion and was sold to Turkey in the same year, and was reclassified as a battery charging hulk in 1973. The two submarines inboard of *Canakkale* are USS *Sea Cat* (SS 399) and USS *Trutta* (SS 421) which was sold to Turkey and became *Cerbe* (S-340) in 1972.

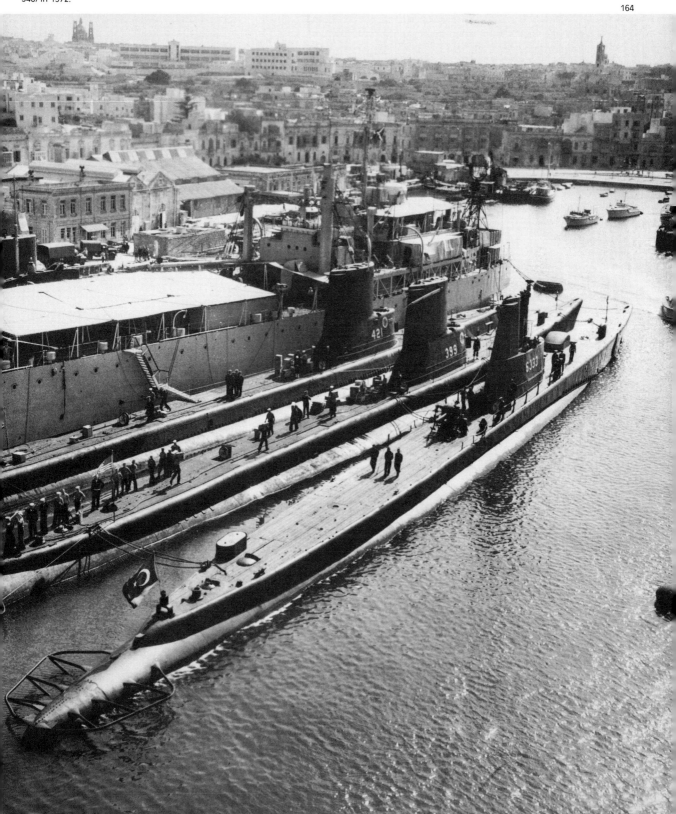

165. Four 'S 70' class submarines, based on the French 'Agosta' class, were constructed by Bazan between 1977 and 1986. Although these boats were built with some French assistance almost 70 per cent of the structural elements and equipment is of Spanish origin. *Galerna* (S 71) is illustrated. (Aldo Fraccaroli)

166. The Turkish Navy has four IKL-designed type 209 submarines, the 'Atilay' class, in service, with a further two under construction. The first three boats were constructed by Howaltswerke, Kiel, and the remaining boats are the first to be constructed in Turkey by Golcuk. This displacement is 980 tons surfaced

and diesel-electric propulsion provides a speed of 10 knots surfaced and 22 knots submerged. A number of ex-US Navy 'Balao' class GUPPY (Greater Under Water Propulsion) conversions were transferred between 1948 and 1972, some of which are still in service.

5

BLANDFORD WAR
PHOTO-FILES

UNION OF
SOVIET SOCIALIST
REPUBLICS

167. Soviet sailors seen during torpedo training aboard what is probably a 'Whiskey' class submarine, in 1957. Submarines had been an important factor in the Soviet Navy before World War Two and continued to be so after 1945. The transformation of the Soviet navy from a coastal defence force to a world-class navy was directly a result of the efforts of

Stalin and Kruschev and Admirals Kuznetsov, Yumashev and Gorshkov, but the competition between the services for funds during the late 1940s was a key issue.

168. A seaman on watch aboard a Soviet submarine in the mid 1950s – probably a 'Whiskey' class boat. At the end of World War

Two the Soviets acquired some ex-German U-Boats – Types IXC, VIIC and XXI – and some of the advances in these designs, particularly the Type XXI, were incorporated into the vessels of the post-war submarine programme. However, Admiral Kuznetsov favoured the bulk ordering of long-lead items for a quantitative rather than a qualitative fleet. He was removed from

167

168

office and was replaced in 1956 by Admiral Gorshkov, now regarded as the architect of the modern Soviet Navy.

169. Two Polish Navy 'Whiskey' class submarines. Two were transferred in 1964 and another two in 1969; only three of these boats now remain in service. About 236 were built –

cut back from the original plan for 340. Transfers were also made to Albania, Bulgaria. China, Cuba, Egypt, Indonesia and North Korea. China constructed about two boats in her own yards.

170. The 'Whiskey Twin Cylinder' class (five boats) were converted 'Whiskey' boats with two missile launchers arranged in parallel, and elevated for firing. One 'Whiskey Single Cylinder' boat appeared in 1956.

171. Six 'Whiskey' submarines were converted to the 'Whiskey Long Bin' class, beginning in 1961. However, to launch their missiles the boats had to surface. The missiles were fitted in the sail, the forward-facing launcher elevating about 14 degrees.

172. A 'Whiskey V' boat being shadowed by the 'Rothesay' class frigate HMS *Rhyl* (F 129). The 'Whiskey' class was built from 1950 to 1957, in five types, at Gorky, Komosomolsk, Leningrad and Nickolaev. Only 53 Type Vs are in service. Two were converted for oceanographic research, *Severyanka* and *Slavyanka*. (Royal Navy)

170

171

173. 'Whiskey' class passing through the English Channel in mid-1974. Displacement is 1,050 tons surfaced, 1,350 submerged. Dimensions are: length 246 ft; beam 20 ft 6 in; and draught 15 ft 9 in. Two Type 37D 2,000 bhp diesels, producing 2,500 shp, give a maximum speed of 17 knots surfaced and 13 knots submerged. Armament consists of six 533 mm torpedo tubes, four bow and two aft, and 12 torpedoes or 24 mines can be carried. The boats have been variously equipped with 57 mm, 25 mm and 100 mm guns. The endurance is up to 45 days and range about 6,000 nm at 5 knots snorkelling. (Royal Navy)

172

173

174. Six 'Whiskey' boats were converted into 'Whiskey Canvas Bag' radar pickets in 1960-61; one is illustrated. Twelve were converted to cruise missile boats in the 1950s. A single-missile carrying 'Whiskey Single Cylinder' was believed to have been converted in 1957, and five 'Whiskey Twin Cylinders' were converted in 1959-61, with 'Whiskey Long Bins' following in 1959-62. The illustration shows a rare view of the Soviet 'Boat Sail' submarine radar installation. A 'Stop Light' broad band passive ECM antenna is forward of 'Boat Sail', with a DF loop further forward. (US Navy)

175. A 'Romeo' class attack submarine. Twenty of this class were built at the Gorky yard between 1958 and 1961. This class was a successor to the 'Whiskey' class with a greater range and two more torpedo tubes. Displacement is 1,330 tons surfaced, 1,700 submerged. Dimensions are: length 252 ft 8 in; beam 22 ft; draught 16 ft. Maximum speed was lower than the 'Whiskey' class being 15.5 knots. Six are in service.

174

176. An early 1960s Soviet propaganda photograph showing a 'Zulu V' boat returning to base after a 'training voyage'. Displacement is 1,900 tons surfaced and 2,350 tons submerged. Dimensions are: length 295 ft 2 in; beam 24 ft 7 in; draught 19 ft 8 in. Maximum speed is 18 knots surfaced and 16 knots submerged. The endurance is 70 days, with a range of 20,000 nm surfaced. Armament consists of ten 533 mm torpedo tubes, six bow and four aft; 22 torpedoes or 44 mines.

177. A 'Zulu IV' conventional attack class submarine. About 32 of this class were built from 1953 to 1955. These were longer range versions of the 'Whiskey' class, seeming to depend more heavily on the Type XXI design. Problems were caused by incorporating components from the German Walther turbines, and they were instead fitted with diesel-electric motors, which delayed operation of the first 12 boats until the mid-1950s. Changes in the appearance of the sail resulted in five variations in the class.

176

177

178. About 30 'Quebec' class attack submarines were launched at Sudomekh yard between 1954 and 1957. They were the third post-war submarine type, a development of the pre-war coastal 'M' class and not a smaller version of the 'Whiskey' and 'Zulu' types. They were designed for Black Sea and Baltic operations and displaced 400 tons surfaced and 540 tons submerged. Dimensions are: length 183 ft 9 in; beam 16 ft 5 in; and draught 12 ft 6 in. Estimated maximum speed was 18 knots surfaced and 16 knots submerged. Armament consisted of four 533 mm torpedo tubes; eight torpedoes were carried. None is thought to remain in service.

179. A 'Foxtrot' class conventional attack submarine photographed, while refueling in January 1975, from a Sea King of No 826 Squadron, RN, from HMS *Tiger* (C 20). Some 62 boats of this long-range development of the 'Zulu' class were completed between 1958 and 1967. Production continues for export purposes. (Royal Navy)

178

179

180

180. A Soviet diver from a 'Foxtrot' class conventional submarine prepares to retrieve a sonobuoy dropped from a NATO maritime reconnaissance aircraft in the Atlantic. The 'Foxtrot' has the distinctive characteristics of a bulbous bow with a sonar dome and a sail with the after part raised. The sail varies from boat to boat. Sensors include a 'Snoop Tray' radar.

The complement is 78 officers and men. (Royal Navy)

181. A 'Foxtrot' class boat photographed south of the Faroes by a Nimrod patrol aircraft of No 201 Squadron, RAF, one of a group of submarines in transit escorted by a 'Don' class submarine support vessel. 'Foxtrot' displaces

1,950 tons surfaced and 2,400 tons sumerged. Dimensions are: length 300 ft 3 in; beam 24 ft 7 in; and draught 19 ft 8 in. Range is 11,000 nm and maximum speed surfaced is 16 knots. Armament comprises six bow and four aft 533 mm torpedo tubes; 22 torpedoes or 44 mines can be carried. (MoD)

182. 'Tango' class conventional attack submarines were built at Gorky at the rate of two per year from 1972 and 19 are in service. This class is a successor to the 'Foxtrot' class and is reported to have a much higher battery capacity and, therefore, much greater endurance. The hulls are sheathed in a sonar-absorbent rubber compound. Armament consists of six 533 mm bow torpedo tubes, and it is believed that the class is fitted for firing the SS-N-15 torpedo tube-launched ASW missile. (MoD)

183. 'Tango' submarines displace 3,000 tons surfaced and 3,700 tons submerged. Dimensions are: length 300 ft 3 in; beam 29 ft 6 in; and draught 23 ft. Machinery consists of diesels producing 6,000 bhp. Maximum speed is 20 knots surfaced and 16 knots submerged. The complement is 72 officers and men. (MoD)

184. The 'November' class nuclear-powered attack submarine *Leninsky Komsomol*, the prototype of her class, was the first Soviet submarine to voyage to the North Pole, travelling under the polar ice pack to surface at the Pole in April 1970, where she is seen in the illustration. The 'November' class was the first Soviet nuclear submarine class, resulting from a decision, if reports are to be believed, made in 1953. Fourteen 'November' boats were built between 1958 and 1965. One boat was lost off Cape Finisterre in April 1970 and another is thought to have been scrapped in 1982-83. Twelve boats are in service.

183

185. 'November' class submarines have streamlined hulls designed for high underwater speed and can reach a speed of 30 knots surfaced. Displacement: 4,500 tons surface, 5,300 submerged. Dimensions: length 363 ft 11 in; beam 29 ft 6 in; and, draught 25 ft 3 in. Armament consists of eight 533 mm bow and four 406 mm stern torpedo tubes. From 26 to 32 torpedoes or mines can be carried. Complement is 80.

186. The 'Golf' class diesel-powered strategic missile submarines were the world's first ballistic missile submarines, each carrying three SS-N-4 missiles inthe fin. These were originally to be large attack boats but plans were altered in the mid-1950s and they were completed as ballistic missile submarines in five versions. A 'Golf II' boat is illustrated.

185

186

187. A displaced 'Hotel II' class nuclear powered strategic missile submarine photographed off Newfoundland in March 1972 by Nimrod reconnaissance aircraft of No 201 Squadron, RAF. The class was designed for firing SS-N-4 missiles but these were replaced by SS-N-5X, which are capable of being launched underwater. Conventional armament consists of six 533 mm bow and 406 mm stern torpedo tubes. Twenty torpedoes are carried. Six boats were completed between 1959 and 1961. All have now had their missile systems disabled in accordance with SALT requirements. (MoD)

188. 'Hotel' class boats, all built at Severodvinsk, displace 5,000 tons surfaced and 6,000 tons submerged. Dimensions are: length 377 ft 4 in; beam 29 ft 6 in; and draught 23 ft. The nuclear reactor produces 30,000 shp giving a submerged speed of 20-25 knots. Complement 80 officers and men. (US Navy)

187

188

189. Five 'Echo I' class nuclear-powered cruise missile submarines were built at Komsomolsk in 1960-62. Originally designed to fire six SS-N-3 missiles, the missile tubes have since been removed from this class. The first of the class has reportedly been configured to perform similar duties to the 'Golf' class command and communications submarines. The remaining six bow 533 mm and four 406 mm aft torpedo tubes suggest that boats still in service will be altered for an attack role. Displacement is 4,500 tons surfaced and 5,500 submerged.
Dimensions are: length 360 ft 11 in; beam 29 ft 10 in; and draught 24 ft 7 in.

190. A disabled 'Echo II' submarine off Newfoundland. An 'Echo II' boat had an internal accident off Okinawa in August 1980, resulting in a number of casualties among the crew, and had to be towed to Vladivostock. This was done through Japanese territorial waters despite Japanese protests. (RAF)

189

190

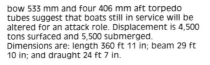

191

191. A total of 29 'Echo II' class nuclear-powered cruise missile submarines were built between 1962 and 1967. This class is a lengthened version of the 'Echo I', the greater length being required to accommodate the extra missile launchers. The antenna mast behind the rail can be laid flat on the deck when not in use. In some boats, the original SS-N-3 has been replaced by SS-N-12 missiles. Other armament consists of six 533 m bow and two torpedo tubes 406 mm aft.

192. 'Echo II' class boats are powered by a nuclear reactor driving two shafts, producing 24,000 shp and giving a speed of 20 knots surfaced and 23 knots submerged. Displacement is 5,000 tons surfaced, 6,000 tons submerged. Their dimensions are: length 377 ft 4 in; beam 29 ft 6 in; and draught 24ft 7 in. The crew consists of 90 officers and men. (MoD)

193. A 'Juliett' class diesel-electric strategic submarine, of which 16 were built at Gorky between 1961 and 1968. The class has six 533 mm torpedo tubes forward and four 406 mm torpedo tubes aft. There are four forward firing missile tubes for SS-N-3A missiles. Originally, boats of this class were divided for duties with the Northern and Pacific Fleets, but more recently four were assigned duties in the Baltic. (Royal Navy)

194. The 'Juliett' class is regarded as a diesel-electric equivalent of the nuclear-powered 'Echo IIs', but with a maximum surfaced speed of 16 knots as opposed to 20 knots in the 'Echo II' boats. The range is 9,000 nm at 7 knots or 15,000 nm at surface cruising speed. Displacement is 3,000 tons surfaced, 3,750 tons submerged. Their dimensions are: length 295 ft 3 in; beam 32 ft 10 in; and draught 23ft. The crew is thought to number 80.

193

194

195. An early photograph of a 'Yankee' class nuclear-powered submarine. Thirty-four were built by the Komsomolsk and Severodvinsk yards between 1967 and 1974. Seven boats have had their missile tubes removed and are now designated as attack submarines. There are six 533 mm bow torpedo tubes and 18 torpedoes are carried.

196. A 'Yankee' class nuclear-powered submarine photographed by a US Navy P-3 Orion surveillance aircraft shortly before sinking. The boat had been on routine patrol some 1,300 miles off the US east coast, 480 miles northest of Bermuda, when one of the sixteen SS-N-6 liquid fuelled ballistic missiles exploded in its silo, resulting in considerable structural damage and ripping a large hole in the external hull just aft of the sail. After the explosion, the boat was taken in tow by a Soviet merchant ship but at only 80 miles from where the boat surfaced, it began to take on water and sank a few hours later. Soviet reports indicate that three crew members were killed and several were injured. (US Navy)

195

196

197. One 'Yankee' class submarine has been refitted with 12 SS-N-17 missiles and is now designated 'Yankee II' (illustrated). It displaces 8,000 tons surfaced and 9,600 tons submerged. Its dimensions are: length 426 ft 6 in; beam 39 ft 4 in; and, draught 29 ft 10 in. Its maximum speed is 27 knots. The complement is 120 officers and men. (DoD)

198. 'Delta I' class strategic submarines are basically a redesign of the 'Yankee' class to accommodate the SS-N-8 missiles. The large bulge abaft the sail is the casing of the missile section, which is higher than in the 'Yankee' class because the SS-N-8 missiles are longer and larger in diameter than the SS-N-6. However, only 12 instead of the planned 16 missiles could be accommodated. About 16 boats were built between 1972 and 1977. The boats displace 9,000 tons surfaced and 11,750 tons submerged. Their dimensions are: 459 ft 4 in; 39 ft 4 in; 28 ft 7 in. The maximum speed of this class is 27 knots. Their complement is 120 officers and men. (MoD)

197

198

199. Four 'Delta II' class strategic submarines were built between 1974 and 1975. The aim was to build a bigger boat to accommodate an extra four SS-N-8 missiles abaft the sail. As a result, underwater speed was reduced to 24 knots. Six 533 mm bow torpedo tubes were fitted, as in all other 'Delta' class variations. They displace 10,000 tons surfaced and 12,750 tons submerged. Their dimensions are: length 508 ft 6 in; beam 39 ft 4 in; and draught 28 ft 10 in.

200. The 'Delta III' class displaces 10,500 tons surfaced and 13,250 submerged. About 14 have been launched from the Severodvinsk yard between 1975 and 1981 in a continuing construction programme. The ugly bulge abaft the sail is larger than in previous 'Delta' types to accommodate the larger SS-N-18 missile. These have a MIRVed warhead and a range of approximately 500 nm.

199

200

201. An artists's impression of a 'Delta IV' nuclear-powered strategic missile submarine launching a MIRVed SS-NX-23 ballistic missile from a break in the Polar ice cap. The first 'Delta IV' was launched in 1984. Three more, with more following, are to emerge from the Severodvinsk yard. The displacement and dimensions are greater than those of the 'Delta II-III' classes, most other particulars are the same. The Russian term for nuclear-powered ballistic missile submarine is *Podvodnaya Lodka Atomnaya Raketnaya Ballisticheskaya*.

202. 'Charlie' class cruise missile submarines were all built at the Gorky yard with 12 'Charlie Is' being built between 1968 and 1973, and five 'IIs' entering service between 1973 and 1981. These submarines are regarded as a follow-on from the 'Echo II' class. As can be seen, one

201

202

improvement was a hull shaped for higher speed and higher performance. The propulsion system can thus be much smaller: a nuclear reactor producing 30,000 shp, giving a maximum speed of 27 knots in 'Charlie Is', which is reduced by one knot in the 'IIs'. (MoD)

203. A 'Charlie' boat photographed passing through the Straits of Singapore on its way to join the Soviet Pacific Fleet. 'Charlie Is' first became operational with eight SS-N-7 missiles; and the later 'Charlie IIs' are fitted with the longer range SS-N-9 missiles. The surface displacement of the 'Charlie Is' is 4,000 tons while that of the 'Charlie IIs' is 4,300. The dimensions of a 'Charlie I' are: length 311 ft 8 in; beam 32 ft 8 in; and draught 26 ft 3 in, but in the case of the 'Chralie IIs' the length is 340 ft.

204. The 'Papa' class cruise missile submarine is a one off design built in 1969-71 and is probably a development of the 'Charlie' class. There are ten tubes for SS-N-9 missiles and four bow torpedo tubes.

205. A 'Victor' class submarine running on the surface at speed. A longer version of the 'Victor I' class appeared in 1972, which was first given the NATO reporting name 'Uniform'. Seven 'Victor IIs' are in service. They are some 500 tons heavier and 30 ft longer than the earlier boats, but 'Victor IIs' are slightly slower than their forerunners. (MoD)

206. The nuclear-powered 'Victor I' class attack boats were the first Soviet submarines to be constructed with an 'Albacore' (tear drop) hull. The gently rounded design of the sail is also intended to produce optimium hydrodynamic efficiency. The maximum speed of the class is about 20 knots. They displace 4,300 tons when surfaced. Their dimensions are: length 311 ft 8

in; beam 32 ft 10 in; and, draught 23 ft. Although seemingly designed for ASW the class also has an anti-ship capability. As well as SS-N-15 missiles armament consists of eight 533 mm bow torpedo tubes and 18 torpedoes are carried. Sixteen 'Victors' are in service.(MoD)

207. About 21 'Victor IIIs' came into service between 1978 and 1985. This class is 20 feet longer and displaces about 100 tons more than 'Victor IIs' and can be recognised by the teardrop-shaped housing for a towed accoustic array sonar on the upper vertical stabiliser. They are reported to have two SS-N-16 missiles and, therefore, two less torpedo tubes than earlier 'Victors'. Note the tandem eight-bladed propeller. (US Navy)

206

207

208. The 'Alfa' class is a high-speed (45 knots) nuclear-powered attack submarine. This is the most streamlined of Soviet submarines, with a deep-diving ability. These titanium-hulled boats have a submerged displacement of 3,700 tons. They are about 260 feet in length. Armament is six 533 mm torpedo tubes; 18 torpedoes or 36 mines are carried. This boat is reported to have SS-N-15 and/or SS-N-16 missiles. 'Alfas' are reported to have liquid-metal-cooled nuclear reactors, which produce higher power compared to pressurised water reactors for the space occupied. Six are in service.

209. Since 1982 two 'Oscar' class nuclear-powered cruise missile submarines have entered service. More are reported to be under construction. This anti-ship submarine can launch its SS-N-15/16 missiles underwater. There are also eight bow torpedo tubes. Their submerged displacement is 14,000 tons and their length is 492 ft.

208

210. Four 30,000-ton 'Typhoon' units are in service with more building. Launched between 1980 and 1984, these 557-ft submarines are designed for operation below ice-cover, as the configuration of the sail indicates, but could operate from any ocean and still be within striking radius of its main targets. The boats are designed with two separate inner hulls covered by the single outer hull with a separation of about six feet between the inner and outer hulls for protection from existing US ASW weapons. The sail is also a separate pressure vessel. (Royal Navy)

211. 'Typhoon', the world's largest submarine, is armed with 20 SS-N-20 solid-propellant missiles with a seven-MIRV capability. Uniquely the missile launch tubes are mounted forward of the sail in a fully integrated weapons area, as can be seen in the artist's impression, which presumably leaves the space abaft the sail for the two reactors. Speed is estimated at 25-30 knots. (Royal Navy)

210

211

212. An artist's impression of the White Sea Severodvinsk submarine production facility, the only major Soviet shipyard on the Arctic coast. 'Typhoon' and 'Delta III' strategic missile submarines and an 'Oscar' class cruise missile boat are depicted. Severodvinsk is the world's largest submarine production yard and is one of five Soviet yards producing submarines.

212

213. Six 'Kilo' class diesel-electric submarines came into service from 1982 onwards, with more building and production running at two per year. The class is probably a successor to the 'Whiskey' and 'Romeo' classes. They displace 2,500 tons surfaced and 3,200 tons submerged. Their length is about 220 ft.

214. One nuclear-powered 'Akula' class attack submarine was launched in July 1984, with another boat reported to be building. Surface displacement is 7,500 tons and length is about 350 ft. The armament comprises torpedoes and SS-N-16/21 missiles.

215. The first of the 'Sierra' class attack boats was launched in July 1983, with another building. Two nuclear pressurised-water reactors, driving a seven-bladed propeller, enable the boat to reach a speed of 36 knots. Their displacement is 6,000 tons surfaced and their length is about 360 ft. Torpedoes and/or SS-N-16/21 missiles are carried.

213

214

215

216. The first unit of the 'Mike' class nuclear-powered attack submarine was launched in 1983, with follow-on boats expected. The hull is constructed from titanium. Their displacement is 5,000 tons surfaced, and their approximate length is 360 ft. Torpedoes and SS-N-15/16/21 missiles are the probable armament.

217. The Soviet submarine-launched SS-NX-21 cruise missile, which as an approximate range of 3,000 km, can be fired from standard submarine torpedo tubes. (US Navy)

216

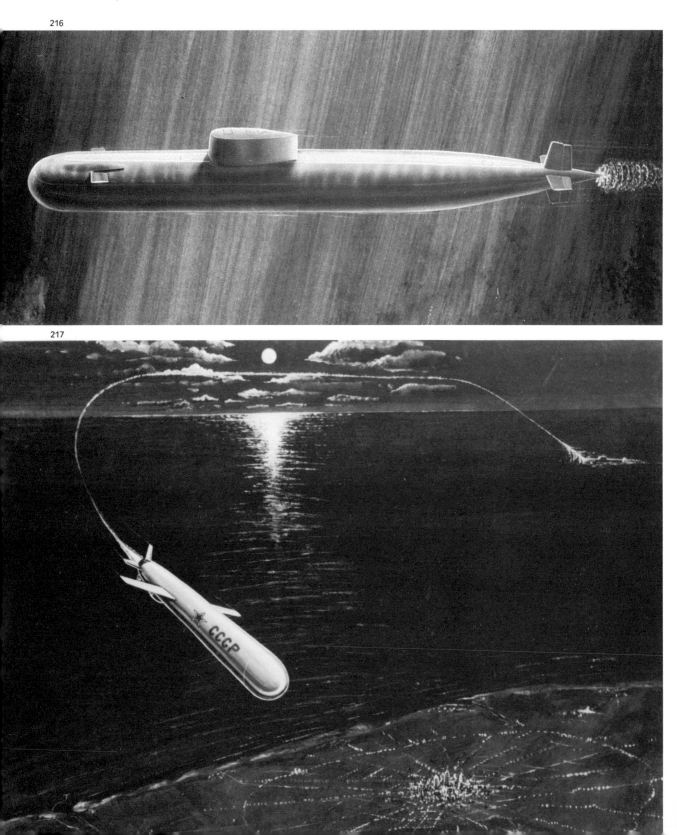

217

BIBLIOGRAPHY

Alden, John D., Commander. *The Fleet Submarine in the US Navy*. Arms and Armour Press. London, 1979.

Almanacco Navale. Rivista Marittima. Rome, various editions.

Bagnasco, Erminio. *Submarines of World War Two*. Arms and Armour Press. London, 1977.

Berg, John. *The Soviet Submarine Fleet: A Photographic Survey*. Jane's Publishing Company. London, 1985.

Brown, Neville, and Farrar-Hockley, Anthony, General Sir. *Nuclear First Use*. The Royal United Services Institute for Defense Studies and Buchan & Enright. London, 1985.

Combat Fleets of the World. Editions J.-C. Lattes. Paris, 1950 to date.

Compton-Hall, Richard. *Submarine Warfare: Monsters and Midgets*. Blandford Press. Poole, 1985.

Conway's All the World's Fighting Ships 1926-1949. Conway Maritime Press. London, 1980.

Conway's All the World's Fighting Ships 1947-1982 (two volumes): *Part 1: The Western Powers; Part 2: The Warsaw Pact and Non-Aligned Nations*. Conway Maritime Press. London, 1983.

Corse, Carl D., Jr. *Introduction to Shipboard Weapons*. United States Naval Institute Press. Annapolis, 1975.

Cowin, Hugh, W. *Conway's Directory of Modern Naval Power 1986*. Conway Maritime Press. London, 1985.

Evans, A.S. *Beneath the Waves: A History of HM Submarine Losses 1904-1971*. William Kimber. London, 1986.

Friedman, Norman. *Submarine Design and Development*. Conway Maritime Press. London, 1984.

Friedman, Norman. *The Postwar Naval Revolution*. Conway Maritime Press. London, 1986.

Galbler, Ulrich. *U-Bootbau*. Verlag Wehr und Wissen. Koblenz and Bonn, 1978.

Hewlett, Richard G., and Duncan, Francis. *Nuclear Navy 1946-1962*. The University of Chicago Press. Chicago, 1974.

Jane's Fighting Ships. Jane's Yearbooks. London, 1945 to date.

Knenne, Robert E. *The Attack Submarine: A Study in Strategy*. Yale University Press. New Haven, 1965.

Leebaert, Derek (ed) *Soviet Military Thinking*. George Allen & Unwin. London, 1981.

Les Flottes de Combat. See Under Combat Fleets of the World.

Lyon, Hugh. *The Encyclopedia of the World's Warships*. Salamander Books. London, 1978.

MaccGwire, Michael (ed) *Soviet Naval Developments: Capability and Context. Papers Relating to Russia's Maritime Interests*. Praeger Publishers. New York, 1972.

Macksey, Kenneth. *Technology in War: The Impact of Science on Weapons Development and Modern Battle*. Arms and Armour Press. London, 1986.

Marriot, John. *Submarine. The Capital Ship of Today*. Ian Allan. London, 1986.

Morris, Eric. *Russian Navy: Myth and Reality*. Hamish Hamilton. London, 1977.

Perspectives upon British Defence Policy 1945-1970. University of Southampton. 1978.

Polmar, Norman. *Atomic Submarines*. D. Van Nostrand Company. New York, 1963.

Polmar, Norman. *Guide to the Soviet Navy*. Naval Institute Press. Annapolis, 1970 to date.

Polmar, Norman. *The American Submarine*. Nautical and Aviation Publishing Company of America. Annapolis, 1983.

Polmar, Norman. *The Ships and Aircraft of the US Fleet*. United States Naval Institute Press. Annapolis, 1978 to date.

Polmar, Norman. *Soviet Naval Power: Challenge for the 1970s*. National Strategy Information Center. New York, 1974.

Preston, Anthony. *The Submarine Since 1919*. BEC Publishing. London, 1974.

Price, Alfred. *Aircraft versus Submarine: The Evolution of the Anti-Submarine Aircraft 1912-1980*. Jane's Publishing Company. London, 1980.

Pugh, Philip. *The Cost of Seapower: The Influence of Money on Naval Affairs from 1815 to the Present Day*. Conway Maritime Press. London, 1986.

Ranft, Bryan, and Till, Geoffrey. *The Sea in Soviet Strategy*. Naval Institute Press, Annapolis, 1983.

Scott, Harriet Fast, and Scott, William F. *The Armed Forces of the USSR*. Westview Press. Boulder, 1984.

Schroeer, Dietrich. *Science, Technology, and the Nuclear Arms Race*. John Wiley & Sons. Chichester, 1984.

Soviet Military Power. US Government Printing Office. Washington, 1981 to date.

The Soviet War Machine. Salamander Books. London, 1977.

Till, Geoffrey. *Maritime Strategy and the Nuclear Age*. Macmillan. London, 1982.

Tsipis, Kosta, Cahn, Anne H., Feld, Bernard T. (eds). *The Future of the Sea-Based Deterrent*. MIT Press. Cambridge, 1973.

The US War Machine. Salamander Books. London, 1978.

Veldman, Jan H., and Olivier, Frits Th. *West European Navies and the Future*. Royal Netherlands Naval College. Den Helder, 1980.

Weyers Flottentaschenbuch. J.F. Lehmanns Verlag. Munchen, various editions.

Whitestone, Nicholas, Commander. *The Submarine: The Ultimate Weapon*. Davis-Poynter. London, 1973.

INDEX

Figures refer to caption numbers.
Names in quotes refer to class names.